THE BOOK THAT FLIES

Alliot Verdon Roe with his No. 1 Avroplane.
This pusher design flew in the Alexandra
Palace competition in London in 1907, where
the *Daily Mail* offered prizes of £250 (about
£30,000 today). A.V. Roe later founded the
Avro company, one of the world's major
aircraft manufacturers, which produced the
Lancaster bomber during the Second World
War.

Mike Hetherington launches his 60-inch
(1,524 mm) span De Havilland Mosquito.
The model weighs 10 ounces (285 g) and
is powered by four rubber motors totalling
2½ ounces (70 g), two in each nacelle, driving
the propellers via gears and effectively
doubling the motor length. The propellers
freewheel after the power is exhausted and
the blades fold back to avoid landing damage.
A timeswitch converted from a miniature
Tomy walking toy motor retracts the
undercarriage.

THE BOOK THAT
FLIES

Building and flying model planes

BOB BASS AND MARTIN DILLY

EBURY
PRESS

Bob Bass is an advertising design consultant. Attending aeromodelling meetings with his two young children re-kindled his own childhood's interest in building and flying model aeroplanes.

Martin Dilly has been an aviation enthusiast all his life. He built his first flying model in 1944. He has been involved since 1960 in the national organisation of model flying with the British Model Flying Association and the Royal Aero Club, and internationally on the Fédération Aéronautique Internationale, where he chairs the information and education committee.

Acknowledgements
Ron Moulton solved several of our problems. David Baker, Mike Colling, Martyn Cowley, Ian Dowsett, Ian Edlin, Alex Imrie, Don Knight, Peter Michel, Jack North and John Stroud provided useful leads. David Cripps performed photographic miracles helped by Paul Westbrook. Phillip Jarrett located obscure photographs. Peter Holland made clear diagrams out of odd sketches. Mick Keates and Martin Illing made the words and pictures fit, with the help of Kay Arlotte at Florencetype. Alan Wiggs built Ajaxes and wrote about building, trimming and tools. Chris Edge wrote the sections on aerodynamics, structures and materials. Ramon Alban wrote about rubber, and John White about ornithopters. Robin James contributed plans and wrote about his unique type of model flying. The hints on getting the best from hand-launched gliders are from Andy Crisp. Adam, David and William Beales built beginners' indoor models and Delta Darts for us. Mike Colling, the British Model Flying Association's education co-ordinator, supplied plans and ideas. Ian Kaynes of Free-Flight News produced computer plots of airfoils. Laurie Barr made numerous five foot flights with an EZB model till David Cripps got the right shot. Models, ephemera and equipment were lent by Terry Dilks, Alan Hardwick, Paul Masterman, John O'Donnell, Russell Peers, Spencer Willis and George Wallbridge of St. Albans Model Supplies. Young flyers Trevor Watts and Tom Norman lent the hands that wind and launch the Delta Darts. Andrew Nahum, curator of the superb aeronautical collection at the Science Museum, London, arranged access to historic models there, while Max Bishop, director-general of the Fédération Aéronautique Internationale, and Sandy Pimenoff, president of the Commission Internationale d'Aéromodellisme, lent international support. Others may never have realised how much they helped, including those who kindly lent models that we were unable to fit into the book.

To Frank Ehling in the United States, who designed the Delta Dart that has introduced three million people already to free-flight, may we add our gratitude and congratulations for a superbly simple idea.

Photography
The special photography for this book was by David Cripps. The sources for other photographs are: via Ramon Alban, 32; Phil Ball, 47; British Aerospace, 13; Martyn Cowley, 28, 50; Martin Dilly, 29, 30, 33, 41, 42, 43, 45, 47, 50, 51, 56, 57, 59, 60, 61, 93, back cover; via Trevor Faulkner, 44; via Mike Hetherington, 3, 60; via Phillip Jarrett, 3, 12, 16, 36, 37, back cover; Keith Miller, 38, 39; via Albert Nazarov, 95; Quadrant Picture Library, 22, 87; Science Museum, London, 13, 14; via John White, 88; Alan Wiggs, 86.

The line drawing on page 17 is by Andrew Crisp, and the illustration on page 90 was provided by British Aerospace.

First published 1993

1 3 5 7 9 10 8 6 4 2

Designed and Produced by Bellew Publishing Company Limited
8 Balham Hill, London SW12 9EA

First published in the United Kingdom in 1993 by
Ebury Press Limited
Random House, 20 Vauxhall Bridge Road, London SW1V 2SA

Random House Australia (Pty) Limited
20 Alfred Street, Milsom Point, Sydney,
New South Wales 2061, Australia

Random House New Zealand Limited
18 Poland Road, Glenfield
Auckland 10, New Zealand

Random House South Africa (Pty) Limited
PO Box 337, Bergvlei, South Africa

Random House UK Limited Reg. No 954009

A CIP catalogue for this book is available from the British Library

ISBN 0 09 178013 6

Printed in Great Britain by Printhaüs Graphique

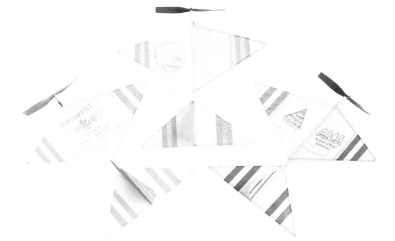

Frank Ehling's Delta Dart design appears round the world in several forms. On the left is the Canadian version, used by the Model Aeronautics Association of Canada in its successful youth programme. Centre is the British Model Flying Association's Dart with red, white and blue covering. On the right is the original Delta Dart, produced by Midwest for the Academy of Model Aeronautics, who have used it since the early 1970s to introduce over two million young people to the world's most popular air sport, model flying.

CONTENTS

THE HISTORY OF EARLY MODEL FLYING

BIZARRE MODELS

WHY AIRCRAFT FLY AND HOW THEY ARE MADE

THE CLASSIC RUBBER MODELS

HIGH PERFORMANCE FREE-FLIGHT

FLYING SCALE MODELS

PREPARATIONS

YOUR FIRST FLYING MODEL

HAND-LAUNCHED GLIDERS

MORE ADVANCED RUBBER MODELS

FLYING FOAM MODELS

UNORTHODOX MODELS

FLYING PRACTICALITIES

CONTACTS AND CONTESTS

BIG EVENTS AND
SMALL BEGINNINGS

There is still romance in flying. Not many people can take it for granted. So, when they see others flying model aeroplanes, they pause to watch, though perhaps with less wonder than those spectators of the earliest attempts to make models fly.

The pioneers of aviation built an extraordinary variety of models to test their theories of flight. They struggled with heavy materials and quite impractical power plants. One small discovery helped: the rubber motor. Uncomplicated, light in weight, it generated considerable power. In a simple way it helped with the experiments that led to the achievement of man's impossible dream: to be able to fly.

Early this century, as aviation developed, so did interest in model flying. Model gliders and rubber-powered aeroplanes were produced by enterprising manufacturers. Most were heavy, with structures of wood and wire covered with fabric, and did not fly very well. Using lighter materials, such as bamboo and silk, groups of enthusiasts created their own designs, and flew them successfully in competitions.

By the late 1920s, international competitions were taking place. A result of this was a new material, introduced from America: balsa wood. It revolutionised model-aeroplane construction. Models could be built very light, yet strong, so they flew longer and better.

Nostalgia in the early days
Even in the late 1940s there was a fascination for the pioneers, their history and the models they flew.

Old model kits are now collectors' items
This box was used to contain a number of different model kits and shows aircraft of the late 1930s. It was discovered, unused, at a jumble sale in 1989. Inside was a kit for a 20-inch rubber-powered model, one of a family produced by the Model Aerodrome in Birmingham during the period. The model, built from the kit plan, has made many flights of over a minute.

Today's classics
The quest for speed, reflected in model aeroplanes and cars, epitomises the spirit and freedom of the time.

Still available
Aeromodeller remains the definitive free-flight magazine, and KeilKraft kits retain enduring popularity. Reprinted *Model Aeronautic Yearbooks*, published in the USA by Frank Zaic, contain myriad sources of inspiration and insight.

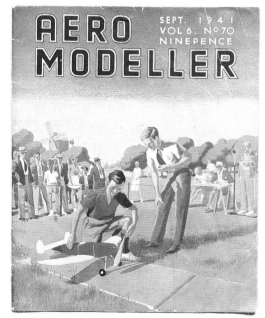

The Golden Era

In the 1930s, civil aviation expanded dramatically; record-breaking aviators – men and women such as Amy Johnson, Wiley Post, Jim Mollison, Charles Kingsford-Smith, Amelia Earhart, Nungesser and Coli – became international celebrities. There was flying fever, and interest in model flying grew with it.

Manufacturers sold plans and kits of successful models. In every town aeroplanes appeared in the model shops, alongside dolls' houses, boats, cars and trains. Aeromodelling magazines were widely read and catalogues scanned for the latest information. Clubs were formed in towns and schools. Local competitions took place and records were established for the longest flights.

People flew gliders, petrol-engined and rubber-powered models. Seaplanes and flying boats took off from ponds. Full-size aircraft were copied as scale models, even with two and four propellers, driven by a complex of whirring gears and rubber motors. Impossibly, some managed to design ornithopters with flapping wings, and succeeded where Icarus had failed.

Invention and experiment flourished: more wings, less wing, a multitude of different shapes and sizes. Conventional models developed aerodynamically and in power. Beautiful models emerged which today are considered classics. By the late 1930s, aeromodelling was flourishing. The art and craft of designing and building became as pleasurable as flying. A model catalogue of the time has the caption, 'The Ideal Hobby for Long Winter Nights and Hazy Summer Days'.

During the Second World War, the use of petrol engines for model aircraft was prohibited, and rubber again became the prime source of power. The modelling magazines of the period give little indication that it was wartime; everything seems unreasonably peaceful. Model flying must have been considered a useful diversion.

Peace in wartime
Gentle competition on the village green. Taking off from makeshift runways, models were timed from 'Rising off Ground'.

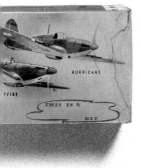

In the 1960s FROG was a major British producer of quality kits and engines. The initials stood for 'Flies Right Off Ground', the sales line for the first ready-to-fly model the company sold in 1932. FROG kits were among the first in Britain to include fully die-cut balsa parts, as opposed to the printed sheet wood supplied by their competitors.

The idea of controlling a model in flight appealed to many, and the advent of digital electronics made this possible. The basic MacGregor radio-control equipment sold for £19 ($26) in 1973 and featured a rubber-driven escapement; this provided full left or right rudder, or neutral.

Jetex motors first appeared in 1948. A small pellet, loaded into a metal casing, produced a jet of gas at a controlled rate when ignited by a wick. Several sizes of Jetex motors were made, the cheapest Atom 35 giving ½ ounce (14 g) of thrust for seven seconds, and costing 22 pence (31 cents). For a couple of decades they were out of production but today several companies make similar motors.

Ups and Downs

Following the end of the war in the mid-1940s, a greater variety of less expensive model aeroplane kits became available. As yet undiverted by the temptations of television, thousands more young people took up the hobby. In the process, they learned the skills of reading plans, of building and assembling models and how to fly them.

It was a time of craft and industry. Miniature diesel and glow-plug engines appeared, mass-produced at accessible prices. Small and very noisy, they were dramatic and exciting. The still air-minded public, recalling the debt they owed to Allied air forces, accepted the occasional distant buzzing in parks and sports fields. Engine-powered models flew faster and higher. Sometimes they crashed heavily and, occasionally, they flew away.

Rubber power was still popular, but during the 1950s engine power gradually took over. Some wanted better control over their models; new electronic technology enabled radio receivers to become smaller and less expensive. They could be readily installed in models powered by diesel engines, but not in the light rubber-powered models. Radio-controlled flying became a success.

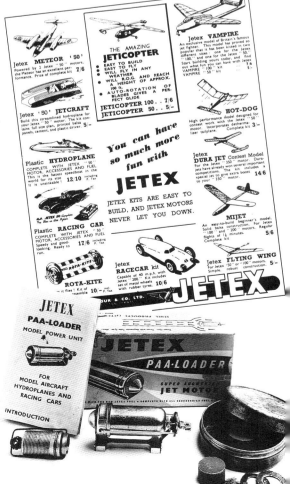

As most of the popular interest in model flying centred round radio-control, rubber as a power source almost faded away. Almost, but not quite.

Some model flyers remained dedicated to the elegant simplicity of the gentle and quiet rubber-powered aeroplanes and gliders, and international competitions continued for free-flight. New designs, materials and techniques were developed, and flight performances became better and better, away from the commercially-driven pressures of radio-flying.

For indoor flying, rubber was, and remains, the main source of power. Gossamer-light models with the thinnest of rubber motors fly for astonishing lengths of time.

Full Circle

What of the old models of the 'Golden Era'? Fortunately, many of the enthusiasts who took up radio control found that, nostalgically, they missed the challenge of flying models in free-flight and returned to their first love. They rediscovered the charm of building and flying the older designs. The odd, the beautiful, the bizarre and sublime models of yesteryear are flying again. Often much improved, all with a special charm, they live happily as a contrast to the exciting new free-flight models of today. With such diversity, the sport and pastime of free-flight remains alive and well. There are now many power sources to choose from: miniature electric and CO_2 motors, compressed air and quiet four-stroke glow-plug engines. Each has its own fascination and devotees, but none has the simplicity of the ubiquitous rubber motor, still the best introduction to model flying.

Eagles and hawks featured in many club badges. Most were produced as waterslide transfers to adorn models and model boxes. The Flying Druids included Stonehenge, while Feltham is today one of Britain's most successful control-line clubs.

In 1949 *Model Aircraft* magazine was 'The Official Journal of the SMAE', Britain's national model flying organisation.

Competition rubber models had to take-off from the ground then, and this tricky moment provided dramatic cover pictures.

Below This rubber motor for a World Championship Wakefield class aeroplane weighs 1.4 ounces (40 g). A loop of ¼ × ¹⁄₂₄ inch (6 × 1 mm) rubber is made into 14 strands about 19 inches (500 mm) long, and drives the propeller for around 35 seconds.

Right Guillow's beginners' free-flight and flying scale model kits, shown in this US ad from the 1960s, are still exported and on sale all over the world.

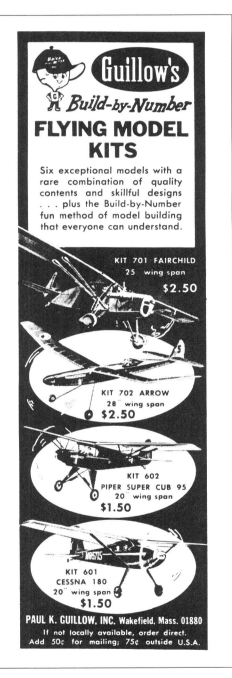

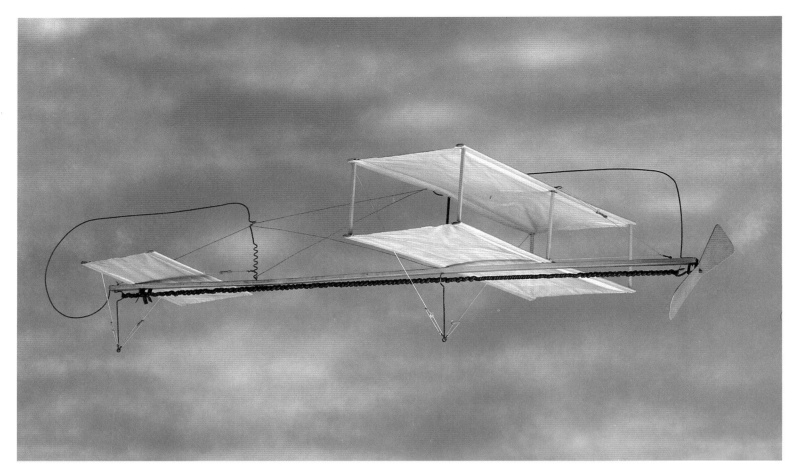

The incidence angle of the Eclipse foreplane or canard was adjustable by sliding the bracing line up or down the zig-zag bends in the wire that also formed the forward bracing post for the wing and a nose bumper for heavy landings. Note the rubber motor under the fuselage stick.

These two reproductions of competition rubber models of the late 1940s were built by vintage-model-aircraft enthusiast Ray Alban. Both were designed to the rules for the World Championship Wakefield Trophy at the time. The upper one is New Look by Jacques Morisset, who was the French champion in 1950. It uses a single-bladed folding propeller, which reduces the drag while the model glides after the rubber power is finished.

The other Wakefield model is Voodoo by Ron Warring, one of the most successful British flyers of the time. It employs a propeller which freewheels at the end of the power run. The bulge under the fuselage houses a parachute which pops out to bring the model safely down after a pre-set time, triggered by a slow-burning fuse. Both aircraft have retractable single undercarriage legs.

CONTRASTS

Early model aircraft were usually driven by rubber-powered pusher propellers (often known then as 'airscrews') at the rear. The Eclipse biplane, left, is typical. It was designed and built by Donald Stevenson around 1909, and was on sale in British toyshops. It is in the collection of the London Science Museum aeronautical department. Its wings are covered with oiled silk and braced with thin cords, tensioned to wire kingposts. It flew from left to right.

The techniques used for early flying models borrow much from model yachting: tensioners on the cord rigging, wire fittings and fabric covering like a sail.

The wingspan of the Eclipse was 25 inches (635 mm) and length 36 inches (914 mm). The designer also sold a model based on the Bleriot cross-Channel monoplane, very much in the public eye at the time. Also in the Science Museum is a box for one of these. On it is written 'Damaged by Winston S. Churchill while flying it with a young relation'. The relation was believed to be the Marquess of Blandford.

Ray Alban prepares to launch his replica of Jacques Morisset's 1950 New Look model. The wing is braced with a wire underneath it, and the undercarriage leg is retracted. In normal contests the model would take-off from the ground.

An indoor rubber-powered flying scale-model of the Hawker Sea Fury fighter, built by Adam Beales. It is to the Peanut Scale rules, which set a wingspan limit of 13 inches (330 mm) and is capable of flights of well over half a minute in a large sports hall. Early model flyer Sir Sidney Camm was responsible for much of the design of the Fury in the mid-1940s.

START SMALL, THINK BIG

In Britain in 1907, flying fever gripped the nation. Just four years earlier, Wilbur and Orville Wright had made man's first successful powered flight in North Carolina, USA. Keen to capitalise on this wave of popular enthusiasm, the press magnate Lord Northcliffe offered £275 in prizes at an indoor competition sponsored by the *Daily Mail* and the Aero Club (later to add 'Royal' to its title).

Almost 7,000 people paid a shilling each to watch 130 model flyers in action indoors. Distance was the aim and a net at the far side of the Great Hall of Alexandra Palace in North London was provided to catch models before they self-destructed on the wall. Power sources included clockwork, rubber, petrol and even gunpowder. For some reason (economy, maybe?) no first prize was awarded, but A.V. Roe took the second place. He flew a 9½-foot (2.9 m) span rubber-powered biplane, with a cane and birch structure covered with tracing paper. The motor came from his brother's braces (suspenders) factory, and the model carried the brand name Bullseye. His longest flight was 30 yards (27.6 m), and he used his winnings to build a manned triplane. Later to form the world-famous Avro aircraft company that produced the Lancaster bomber, he was knighted as Sir Alliot Verdon Roe.

Other initiators in aviation who were model flyers include Sir Richard Fairey, Sir Thomas Sopwith, Sir Frederick Handley-Page, Sir Geoffrey de Havilland and Sir Sidney Camm, designer of the Hawker Hurricane fighter. All were members of the Kite and Model Aeroplane Association, forerunner of the British Model Flying Association, the world's oldest model flying organisation. Later model flyers included Sir Frank Whittle in the UK, who pioneered the gas turbine engine, and Neil Armstrong in the USA, the first man on the moon.

The Avro Company, founded by Sir Alliot Verdon Roe, built the Lancaster bomber of the Second World War. This Merlin-engined Mark I has a housing for the H2S radar bombing equipment under the fuselage. The last aircraft type built by Avro was the Vulcan four-jet delta-winged bomber. Shown here is the prototype. The Mark I Vulcan entered RAF service in 1957, and later versions were still flying in the mid-1980s.

The first aircraft built by Alliot Verdon Roe was this canard biplane, later fitted with a third wing, to become a triplane. Although a four-bladed propeller is installed here, the aircraft, probably photographed at the Brooklands race car circuit, lacks the French-made Antoinette engine which later powered it.

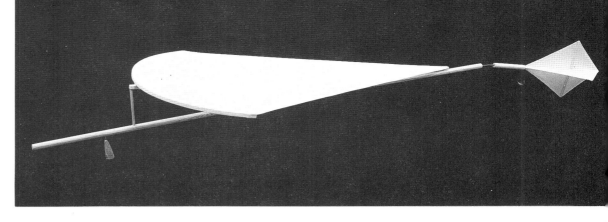

Sir George and the Drag

A century before that early competition in London, a Yorkshire landowner, Sir George Cayley, laid the foundations of flight. He sensibly avoided the pitfall of trying to flap into the air, and instead studied kite flight. He decided that instead of letting the wind push against the kite to keep it airborne, it ought to be possible to reverse the process. He replaced the kite's string with a weight, and added a rigid, but adjustable tail to stabilise the device. In his own words:

> A common paper kite containing 154 square inches was fastened to a rod of wood at its hinder end and supported at its forepart from the same rod by a peg, so as to make an angle of 6 degrees with it. This rod proceeded on behind the kite and supported a tail made of two planes crossing it at right angles, containing 20 square inches each. This tail could be set at any angle with the stick.

Sir George had thus produced an ideal research device. It was simple, and various features – the angle of the wing, the position of the nose weight, the horizontal and vertical angles of the tail – could all be adjusted to give the best performance. He discovered the importance of carefully shaping the *rear* part of an object moving through the air to reduce its wind resistance, or drag, and he investigated streamlining. Most importantly, he published his results in *On Aerial Navigation* so other experimenters could learn from them.

Although existing engines lacked the high power/weight ratio needed for flight, Cayley realised that the essential principle of powered flight was 'to make a surface support a given weight by the application of power to the resistance of air'.

La Route Française

Fifty years after Cayley flew his glider, a French naval officer, Felix du Temple, successfully flew a steam-powered model aircraft, and designed a man-carrying version,

Above A replica from London's Science Museum Aeronautical of Sir George Cayley's 1804 glider, based on a kite, but fitted with a cruciform tailplane and fin and an adjustable nose weight. The results of his tests with this aircraft laid the foundations of later aeronautical developments.

Right An early annotated sketch of Alphonse Penaud's Planophore rubber-powered pusher model, which first flew in 1871 in Paris, and was later widely sold in department stores.

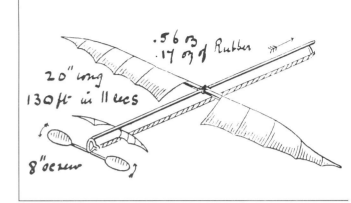

complete with a splendid funnel. Later, this *did* leave the ground, though only after an extended downhill trundle along a ramp.

Still in France, where enthusiasm for aviation is a way of life, Alphonse Penaud flew a rubber-powered model aircraft in the Tuileries Gardens in Paris in 1871, and caught the imagination of his nation. His 18-inch (460 mm) model used a pusher propeller, at the rear, rather than the tractor type we know today. It weighed 0.56 ounces (16 g) and was powered with 0.17 ounces (5 g) of rubber. The blades of its 8-inch (200 mm) propeller were cut from feathers, and it was designed to be inherently stable, essential for any free-flight aircraft where no external control is possible.

The Planophore flew stably for 131 feet (40 m) and stayed airborne for 11 seconds. Penaud sold several hundred flying models like this to eager Parisians. Although his work was denigrated by some contemporaries, his achievement was a landmark, and he is today remembered by the trophy bearing his name, awarded to the top-scoring team at the World Championships for rubber-powered aircraft.

Sidney (later Sir Sidney) Camm (second from left) and a group of smartly-outfitted model flyers in Windsor Great Park around 1910. Most of the aircraft are pusher canards (i.e. tail-first) but the man on the right has not only an elegant bowler hat, but also an advanced-looking tractor type with an orthodox tail.

MR CLARKE AND HIS FLYERS

The T.W.K. Clarke Company set up in business in Kingston, south-west of London, in 1908, close to the site where a new factory set up by Thomas Sopwith would soon be producing Camels and Pup biplane fighters for the Royal Flying Corps. That same factory later became Hawker Aircraft, the centre for Hurricane production during the Battle of Britain, and finally British Aerospace, producing Harriers until it closed in 1992.

Mr Clarke was less ambitious. His Patent Flyers came in four sizes, from 3 feet (914 mm) long down to 12 inches (305 mm). The largest were capable of flights of over 400 feet (120 m) and were powered with 12 strands of ⅛ inch (3 mm) square rubber, turning a carved pusher propeller with very spoon-like blades, that could pop off its shaft to prevent breakage in hard landings. The big Flyers weighed 20 ounces (570 g), and the wings were cambered and carved from cedar wood.

Mr Clarke used an early version of the delayed propeller start now employed by many of today's World Championships competition rubber-powered aircraft. The weight of the Flyers meant they had to fly fast in order to produce sufficient lift to stay airborne, so a hard throw was needed for the launch. After winding the rubber motor, the pusher propeller was locked stationary by a pin attached to a string on the launcher's wrist. As he threw the Flyer, the pin stayed behind, allowing the propeller to start.

The Clarke A flyer was all-wood and had a solid cedar wing that could be slid fore and aft on the fuselage to adjust the flight. Wingspan was 5 feet (1,538 mm) and length 3 feet (924 mm). The propeller, shown on bottom left, sprung off its shaft in a heavy landing. The direction of flight was from left to right.

The Flyer shown right is from London's Science Museum, and has the twin fuselage spars used on most that were sold. However, the Flyer that Mr Clarke is about to launch in the photograph above seems to have a single fuselage spar, with the rubber underneath. The heading photograph shows all models with the rubber motor above the canard foreplane, which might help to prevent the motor collecting too much harmful grit on landing.

FLYING A KITE AND TAKING A DIVE

Almost 3,000 years ago, around 1000 BC, the Chinese were flying kites. Luckily for kite flyers, China had either invented or grew materials useful for early aerospace activities: bamboo, rice paper and silk. These had the important quality of combining comparatively high strength with low weight, vital if you are trying to make something intended to fly. One man, Mo Tzu, worked for years on an all-wood kite, but apparently early flight trials ended when the wooden wonder was destroyed in a crash, and the lighter materials held the day. In Europe there were no such materials, so parchment, leather, feathers and cloth were tried instead.

UP DOWN UNDER

Enthusiasm for advancing the state of the art in aviation, still alive in competition model flyers today, was worldwide in the late nineteenth century. In New South Wales, Australia, Lawrence Hargrave used rubber power successfully to operate flapping-wing models. His wings had a stiff spar at the front, but the wing surface was flexible so, as the spar beat up and down, the twisting wing produced a forward thrust. Hargrave is remembered today in Australia on the $20 banknote, which shows some of his models.

U.S. SUCCESS

At the beginning of the twentieth century aviation was still an infant science. Round the world, much of the research was done with models, and many of the model flyers went on to become famous names in aviation.

Clubs sprang up and competitions were organised, often heavily sponsored by newspapers. At first distance rather than duration was the aim. At the 66th Street Armory, near Broadway in New York, the New York Model Aero Club (NYMAC) held its first contest in 1907; before long, many entrants' models, rubber-powered, were hitting the far wall 200 feet (61 m) away. NYMAC moved to Staten Island to share Oakwood Heights airfield with the Wright Model Bs and the Curtis Pushers that were the state-of-the-art in full-sized flying.

A-Frame Up

Just before and after the First World War, the design of choice was the A-frame pusher. The drawing explains the name. The aircraft, described as the Schweitzer Duration Model, held the US record at 230.8 seconds. The wingspan was 26½ inches (673 mm), and the two 10-inch (255 mm) propellers rotated in opposite directions to cancel out the tendency of the rubber torque to roll the model in flight.

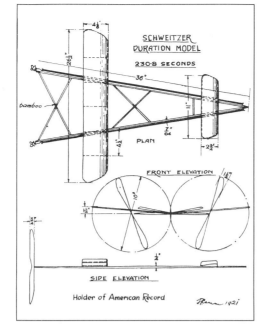

Mann & Grimmer in Britain and the Ideal Model Airplane and Broadfield Billings companies in the USA sold similar models through major toyshops. Materials such as piano wire, oiled silk, birch and spruce formed the structure, and flights of several hundred yards were possible.

Lifting the Load

In Britain, just before the First World War, the Kite and Model Aeroplane Association ran a popular series of weight-lifting contests for rubber-powered aircraft. The rules required the models to weigh at least 1 pound (453 g) and to be able to rise from the ground under their own power when carrying a dead-weight payload of a quarter of the model weight. The minimum qualifying flight duration was 15 seconds, but one model managed a flight of nearly 70 seconds.

The three-view drawing right shows one of these weight lifters, though the designer is unknown. It comes from a 1920 copy of the long-vanished magazine *Everyday Science*. Its wingspan was 4 feet (1.22 m) and great emphasis was put on reinforced joints, carefully pinned and glued, and sometimes with brass plates to support highly-stressed parts. With a flying weight of at least 1¼ pounds (556 g), a lot of thrust was needed to get the thing airborne, and this came from twin motors, geared together to drive the 15-inch (380 mm) propeller. The article quotes these as each being nine strands of ¼-inch (6 mm) rubber, but this was probably square

A Twining A-frame pusher model flying in Britain around 1912. For some reason it is using only one rubber motor and propeller, instead of the usual two.

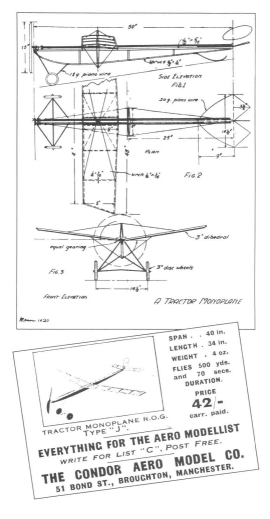

A TRACTOR MONOPLANE

TRACTOR MONOPLANE R.O.G.
TYPE "J".

SPAN . . 40 in.
LENGTH . 34 in.
WEIGHT . 4 oz.
FLIES 500 yds.
and 70 secs.
DURATION.
PRICE
42/-
carr. paid.

EVERYTHING FOR THE AERO MODELLIST
WRITE FOR LIST "C", POST FREE.
THE CONDOR AERO MODEL CO.
51 BOND ST., BROUGHTON, MANCHESTER.

An advertisement from the August 1920 British magazine *Everyday Science* for the Type J Rise-Off-Ground Tractor Monoplane, very expensive at 42 shillings.

section, rather than flat as at present. Holding the model while winding was in progress was probably not a popular task with fellow flyers.

Lighter is Better

Meanwhile, in 1910, an American, Armour Selley, was experimenting with a new material from South America. It was balsa wood, with a density from as little as 4 lb/ft³ (0.06 gm/cm³). He flew models made from this to break several records, flying for two-thirds of a mile (1.07 km) at a height of about 40 feet (12 m). Balsa was later to revolutionise the sport of model flying.

In the USA things stagnated a bit after the First World War, but Charles Lindbergh's solo crossing of the Atlantic in 1927 fired enthusiasm again. Shortly after, a contest in California attracted over 1,000 model flyers, and in 1931, even at the height of the Depression, the Airplane Model League of America had 425,000 members.

International Contests

The same year that Lindbergh, known before his success as the Flying Fool, made his epic flight, the director of a British oil company, Sir Charles Wakefield (later Lord Wakefield of Hythe), donated a trophy for the world's first international model flying contest. Today, the Wakefield Trophy is model-flying's most sought-after award. It is restricted to rubber-powered free-flight aircraft, and recent winners have included flyers from North Korea, the former USSR, the USA and Germany.

In those early days compressed-air power was used, as well as rubber, and English flyer D.A. Paveley took second place in 1929 with this type of motor. The other competitors used small, fast-turning propellers driven by several rubber motors geared together, and the usual spruce, wire and silk construction and covering. Today, with the focus on green power, commercial compressed-air motors are again appearing, but using a modified plastic fizzy drinks bottle as an air reservoir, instead of the laboriously wire-bound, soldered brass tanks used in the 1920s.

The next year Joe Earhart arrived from the USA and revolutionised the event, winning with a light model built from balsa and covered with tissue paper. A single skein of rubber turned a large propeller slowly, at

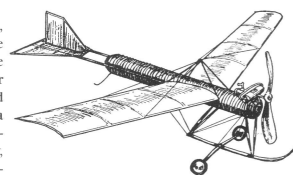

A typical compressed-air-powered model of the 1920s.

about 450 rpm. He also used a technique still employed today: he wound the motor while it was stretched to about five times its normal length. This both allows more turns to be put on and also preserves the rubber.

Competition flying improved the breed, and technical developments followed fast. Propellers that free-wheeled after the rubber power was exhausted reduced the drag; later improvements made the blades fold back along the fuselage sides. More rubber was packed into lighter airframes but, of course, there was a limit after which the stored energy in the motor would collapse the fuselage instead of turning the propeller. Some people reverted to geared motors, but this time to increase the motor-running duration.

Balsa logs being carried in Ecuador in the 1920s. The same wood was used for Thor Heyerdahl's trans-Pacific raft, the *Kon Tiki*.

FUN WHEN YOU KNOW HOW

Today, after years of experiment and the gaining of knowledge, allied to the introduction of new materials and lighter weight power sources, free flight model flying has never been so varied, as this book shows. However, the majority of models are designed to fit the established convention of what an aeroplane looks like. But, if the principles of why and how an aeroplane flies are well understood, need this be so? This question is asked by the designer and builder of the models on these pages.

Robin James challenges the rules, and his models are a wonderful example of the creative freedom gained from a thorough understanding of aerodynamic principles. Surprising, unconventional, all these models make good use of lightweight materials and clever design. Above all, they fly well and are an inspiration, particularly to the young. They live up to Robin's belief that model flying should be seen to be fun.

Believe it or not, there are sound technical reasons why this model looks like a Venetian blind. It was designed to fly in a small hall only 25 feet (7.5 m) wide. Two things are needed to make a model turn tightly; one is a slow flying speed and the other is a small wingspan. With the weight of a motor to carry, the design solution was to use short wings and plenty of them, thereby generating a lot of lift and drag. This little quintuplane flies excellently in tight circles, hence its name – Whoopee! It can be powered by electric, CO_2 or rubber motors, and plans are available from SAMS.

This 'flying box' turns heads everywhere; the impossible flies! Most people who see it think 'That shouldn't fly' or 'where are the wings?'. In fact, the wings are at the centre and the fuselage at the sides, a highly original arrangement. What is more, there are two wings, so it is a biplane. The tailplanes are the same size as the wings, therefore it is a tandem winged biplane! The 12-inch (300 mm) square box flies in a very stable manner and indoors takes off and lands perfectly on its wheels. Construction is almost exclusively of 3 mm thick polystyrene foam sheet, and power is provided by a commercially available Knight & Pridham KP-01 electric motor.

CATCH THEM YOUNG

The average age of British model flyers has been steadily rising over the past twenty years. One reason is that children are the target of some very hard selling of consumer entertainment and fashion-related products intended to be obsolete in a short time. Peer pressure results in the majority following the latest trends; such trends do not usually involve making much effort, and instant gratification is not a part of model flying. Radio-controlled flying has been heavily promoted by the trade and is often regarded by the public as the only type of model flying today. Nothing could be further from the truth.

To attract young people and to stop the drift, the BMFA launched an education programme in the late 1980s, with its own version of the Dart, similar to the one with this book, as the core model. It links with the national curriculum used in schools, and the Teachers' Guide shows how building and flying the Dart and other basic model aircraft helps pupils to understand aerodynamics, as well as giving a purpose to maths, physics, craft and technology.

Write for more details of this exciting scheme to:
Education Programme, BMFA, Chacksfield House, 31 St Andrews Road, Leicester LE2 8RE.

Looking more like a spaceship than an aeroplane, this dramatic and unconventional model truly lives up to its name – Wotsit. It flies well and fast, rolling continuously to the left while circling to the right. Each of its three 'wings' has a twist to create the roll, and counterbalanced elevators, or more correctly 'elevons', for stability in pitch. Built from various types of plastic foam, with balsa spars for rigidity, it has thin nylon rigging to keep the light structure in place. Each wing is 10½ inches (270 mm) long, the model uses a moulded plastic propeller and power comes from a rubber motor.

Not quite to scale, with larger fins than normal, these amusing models are part of a shoal of fish created by Robin James. Built in various sizes and gaily decorated, they cruise gently round and give the term 'flying fish' a new meaning. The pair shown here have a 'finspan' of 17 inches (432 mm) and 9½ inches (241 mm), are constructed from polystyrene foam wall insulation and powered by rubber motors.

Inspired by a less than cloudless sky, this particular 'cloud' drifts gently through the air in leisurely circles. The multiple lifting and vertical surfaces provide good stability and the egg-box-like construction of foam sheet makes the model very robust. This particular model spans 11½ inches (292 mm) and is 14 inches (355 mm) long. Powered by a KP-01 electric motor, flight times are up to three quarters of a minute.

FORCES IN FLIGHT

Like a fish in water, an aeroplane, model or man-carrying, moves through the substance that keeps it up – the air. Take away the air and it would drop like a brick.

To fly, aeroplanes must generate *lift*, as gravity will always try to pull them down because of their *weight*. They need power, or *thrust*, to move them forward as the air tries to *drag* them back. They need stability in three dimensions because, unlike a car or a boat, they can move up and down, as well as sideways and forwards.

Model aeroplanes in free-flight, with no remote control, need inherent stability built into their design. To help understand this we need to look at why and how they fly.

An aeroplane, unlike a hot-air or a gas-filled balloon, is heavier than the air it flies in, though the air itself is surprisingly heavy. A cubic yard weighs just over 2 pounds (a cubic metre weighs 1.23 kg). How that aeroplane flies depends on the four forces that act on it: thrust, drag, weight and lift.

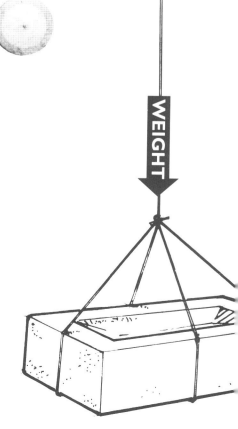

THRUST

Any model aeroplane needs thrust to move it forwards through the air. Most use an engine – petrol, diesel, rubber or gas turbine. A glider employs the force of gravity as thrust, and will always move downwards with respect to the air it flies in, once free of its tug or its towline, though its wing ensures that it flies forwards too.

An efficiently-designed aeroplane will need far less thrust to fly, and thus can climb higher, stay up longer or fly further.

LIFT

Lift allows model aeroplanes to fly. To generate lift aeroplanes must have wings and fly forwards. This forward airspeed is essential to produce a difference between the air pressures above and below the wing. Lower pressure on top of the wing effectively sucks the aeroplane upwards.

The amount of lift produced by the wing and tail depends on the surface's area, the efficiency of the cross section, or airfoil, chosen for it, the angle it makes with the airflow and the speed of the aeroplane. As the wing has much greater area than the tailplane, it produces the most lift.

DRAG

Drag can be thought of as air resistance. Stick your hand out of a moving car, palm forwards, and you will feel the air force it back. The faster the car goes, the greater will be that force. That is drag. Try turning your hand so the palm is horizontal; it is now causing much less drag, because its frontal area is reduced, and you can feel it is being forced backwards much less. If you bend down over the handlebars of a bicycle you find it easier to peddle; less drag means you need less power to move at the same speed.

Aircraft designers go to great lengths to reduce drag to improve performance. Drag depends on the shape of an object moving in air, as well as its area; a more streamlined shape will have less drag than a blunt one, even of the same frontal area. This is why cars are carefully shaped at the back, as well as the front. On model aircraft exactly the same rules apply. Designers smooth fuselages to minimise drag. Roger Ruppert's modern Wakefield on page 27 and William Beales's on page 46 have much less 'draggy' fuselages than the big boxy one required by the rules when Dick Korda's Wakefield on pages 38/39 was designed in 1939.

WEIGHT

Light model aeroplanes fly better than heavy ones, as long as they are strong enough. Excess weight requires either more lift or more thrust to keep the aeroplane flying, so every part of an aeroplane, model or man-carrying, must pull its weight, or rather must carry it. Birds have evolved along the same principles; that is why they have tubular bones instead of almost solid ones as we do.

KEEPING UP

As a wing moves forwards, the air is split and moves over the top and bottom surfaces. The shape of the airfoil makes the air move a greater distance over the highly curved top surface and as a result it moves faster. The air moving over the lower surface has less distance to travel and doesn't need to move as quickly. The effect of the speed difference is a reduction of pressure on the top compared to the bottom, and this lowering of pressure sucks the wing upwards; this effect is called lift.

The lift produced on a wing changes across the section width, or *chord*, from front to rear of the wing. The highest lift force occurs at about a quarter of the chord, and at this point the internal loads in the wing are greatest. It is common, therefore, to position spars here along the wingspan to stop this load breaking the wing.

ANGLE OF INCIDENCE

The greater the angle of the airfoil to the airflow (the angle of incidence), the more lift will be generated, but beyond a certain angle the air can no longer follow the airfoil and starts to break away from the top surface. With more incidence the air will no longer be attached to the top surface and, suddenly, all the lift force is lost. This point is known as the stall. As an aircraft approaches the stall the drag increases sharply and, as a consequence, the speed reduces until the stall occurs and the aircraft falls out of the sky.

ASPECT RATIO

The aspect ratio of a wing can also have a significant effect on the wing efficiency and hence on the duration of the flight. Aspect ratio is the span of the wing divided by its chord, and higher aspect ratios cause less drag. An extreme case is the Voyager aircraft, below right; only the efficiency of its

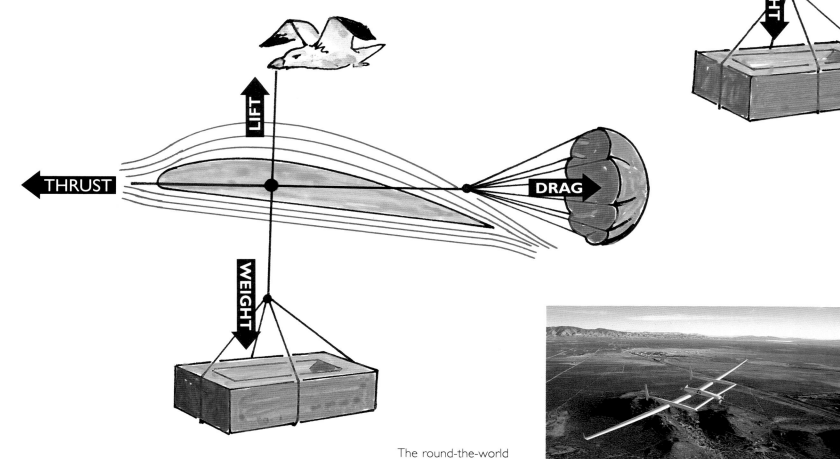

The round-the-world Voyager aircraft was designed by former model flyer Bert Rutan

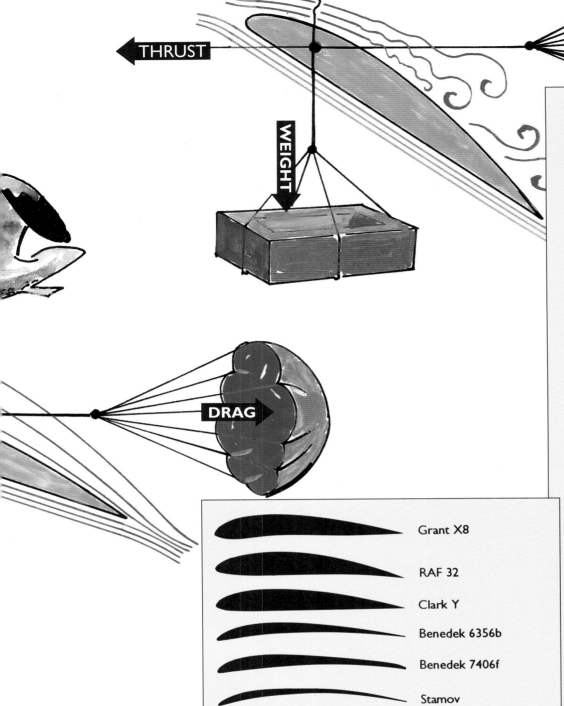

THRUST

WEIGHT

DRAG

DRAG

Grant X8

RAF 32

Clark Y

Benedek 6356b

Benedek 7406f

Stamov

extremely high aspect ratio wing enabled it to fly non-stop round the world without refuelling. Wings like this are designed to bend in flight, and in fact this gives a smoother ride. Next time you fly in a passenger aircraft, look out of the window at a wingtip, and notice how the whole wing flexes if the aircraft is flying through turbulent air.

Aerobatic aircraft and interceptor fighters must be very manoeuvrable, and this puts very high stresses on the wings; a low aspect ratio makes sure they don't snap off when the aircraft turns tightly.

There is a practical limit to aspect ratio as, with a restricted wing area, the chord will become small, the span enormous and the structure will be impossible to build.

CAMBER

The thickness and curvature of an airfoil section, known as its camber, has a significant effect on its efficiency. Generally, thinner, more cambered airfoil sections give more lift and less drag than the thicker, less cambered ones. This is why these airfoils are used on modern competition models.

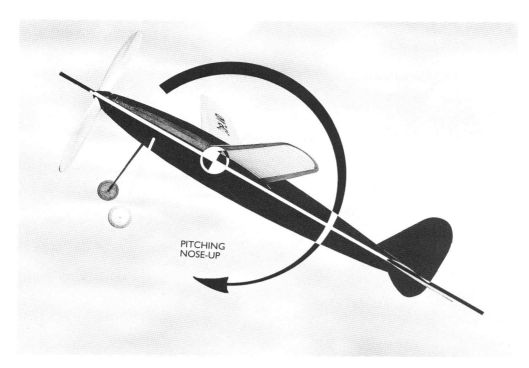

PITCHING
NOSE-UP

PITCH

When the nose of an aeroplane moves up or down into a climb or a dive, this is a change in its *pitch* attitude. The tailplane helps to stabilise the aeroplane in its horizontal attitude.

The lift produced by a wing or tailplane depends on its angle of incidence. To ensure that an aircraft is stable in pitch, the wing and tailplane are set at slightly different angles of incidence; when the aircraft flies forwards the combined effect is to balance the two lift forces at a particular flying speed. It is then said to be 'trimmed'.

Model flyers adjust the wing and tail incidences to trim an aircraft

STEADY AS SHE GOES

Unless an aeroplane is stable, the pilot will constantly have to correct disturbances caused to its flight by gusts and turbulence in the air. A free-flight aeroplane has no pilot, so *must* be inherently, or automatically, stable in order to return to an even keel on its own if disturbed. It needs stability round three axes, *pitch*, *roll* and *yaw*.

CENTRE OF GRAVITY

An aeroplane can rotate round three axes passing through its centre of gravity (the CG). This is the point at which the aircraft balances horizontally and where its total weight acts downwards. On model aircraft the CG is usually roughly midway along the fore and aft width (called the 'chord') of the wing, and its precise position is critical to the way the aeroplane flies.

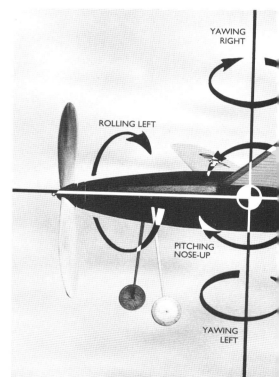

YAWING
RIGHT

ROLLING LEFT

PITCHING
NOSE-UP

YAWING
LEFT

ROLL

Roll stability is necessary to prevent an aircraft rotating round the axis of its fuselage. It is obtained by dihedral, or angling the wingtips upwards, or else by angling the wings backwards; the Delta Dart uses both of these methods.

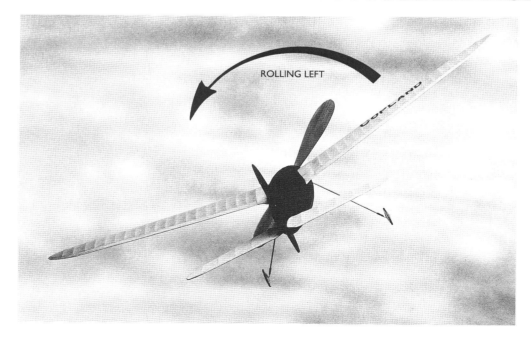

ROLLING LEFT

and also move the CG along the chord of the wing. In fact, they will adjust the position at which the CG lies on the wing, either by adding weight to the nose or tail or by moving the wing slightly forwards or backwards.

For the best performance, a free-flight model must fly close to the stalling speed, but not too close, otherwise it *will* stall if upset by a gust, and duration will be lost. If the tailplane is giving too much lift or the model is too nose-heavy it will dive, and again duration will be lost. Flyers usually adjust a model to just stop the stall, obtain the best performance and so provide some pitch stability.

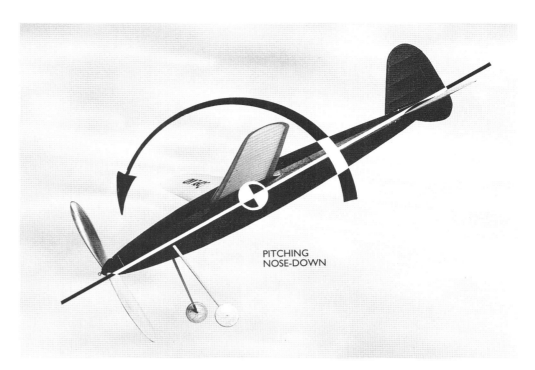

PITCHING NOSE-DOWN

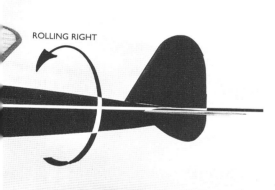

ROLLING RIGHT

YAW

Yaw stability is necessary to keep the aircraft flying in the right direction, with the nose at the front. To achieve this, you need a vertical sideways lifting surface, called a *fin*, near the back of the aircraft. Arrows and darts have fins for the same reason, which is why they always fly in one direction.

Although we usually think of lift as being produced by a wing, and therefore acting upwards, the fin of an aeroplane is really just a small vertically-mounted wing, designed not to produce its lift (now sideways acting) unless the whole aeroplane is disturbed around the yaw axis.

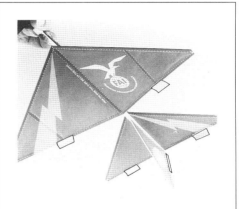

CONTROL AND VARIATIONS

The *rudder*, *elevator* and *ailerons* locally affect the lift produced on the fin, tailplane and wing respectively. These are used to manoeuvre the aircraft in yaw, pitch and roll. On free-flight aircraft, like the Delta Darts you will be building, pre-set trim tabs are sometimes used instead.

You can think of these adjustable tabs or movable inset surfaces as acting to alter slightly the camber of the wing or tailplane to which they are attached. In the case of ailerons, which are near the tips of a wing, they move in opposite directions. As one is moved up the other goes down, reducing the camber and lift on one wing and increasing them on the other; this produces a roll.

On a manned aircraft the pilot moves the rudder with his feet on rudder pedals. Moving the control column backwards or forwards alters the elevator position, while a sideways movement controls the ailerons.

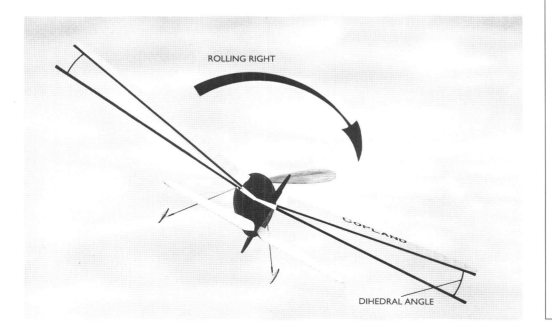

ROLLING RIGHT

DIHEDRAL ANGLE

TAKING THE LOAD

Considerable differences of pressure, or load, are exerted on an aeroplane as it flies. The structure of an aeroplane must be designed to resist the loads generated by lift and landing forces, among others. Where forces are greatest we need the most strength and stiffness, which can be provided by a large area of wood or a small area of composite material.

Wing and Tailplane Structures

Spars are used to resist bending and shear caused by the aerodynamic lift forces, and can be quite large in section. Leading and trailing edge members provide strength against hitting objects and to help form the ends of the airfoil section. Sometimes, as in Roger Ruppert's Wakefield, a combination of leading edge and mainspar is used, joined by a thin skin of Kevlar (see page 28) to form a D-shaped box. This makes a wing that resists twisting very well, yet is lightweight.

To form the rest of the airfoil section, ribs are used, typically from thin balsa wood. The wing covering forms the airfoil section between the ribs and may also provide additional torsional stiffness. Roger's model uses stiff carbon-fibre strips glued on the top and bottom of each rib and a covering of very thin transparent Mylar plastic.

Swiss flyer Roger Ruppert uses composite materials like carbon and Kevlar cloth to stiffen the structure of his 1992 World Championship class F1B Wakefield without increasing the weight as traditional materials would. The wing is covered with Mylar film, over a structure using a very thin moulded carbon D-shaped leading edge box. This prevents the wing from 'fluttering' during a very hard launch.

The fuselage is a carbon and Kevlar tube; it will withstand a fully-wound rubber motor breakage. The wing spans 61 inches (1,564 mm) and the aircraft weighs 8.2 ounces (230 g), including the 1.4-ounce (40 g) rubber motor.

Dick Korda's 1939 Wakefield winner used a traditional all-balsa structure. The fuselage has four longerons running its full length to resist the tension of the wound rubber. Spacers are used to form the overall shape and to stop the longerons buckling. When the covering of taut tissue is added it gives torsional stiffness to resist the twisting forces of the rubber motor. Diagonal wood bracing could improve this further.

Fuselage Structures

For rubber-powered models, the fuselage needs to be strong in compression to take the tension of the rubber motor, strong and stiff in torsion to take the twisting action of the rubber motor when fully wound and locked before launch, and able to take impact loads in case the rubber breaks.

For many modern rubber models, composite tube fuselages are used. Early tubes were made from glass composite, but were soon replaced by Kevlar cloth tubes which are much better under impact and weigh less. Alternative tubes incorporate balsa covered in glass, carbon or Kevlar cloth.

Today, composite fuselage tubes have also replaced the traditional wood structures for gliders.

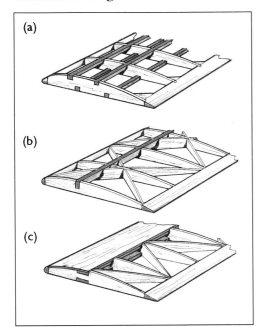

(a) This wood wing structure has several small-section spars and triangular gussets to reinforce the joint at the shallow rear end of each rib.

(b) This wing has a single deep mainspar with diagonal ribs – the so-called Union Jack structure – and resists twisting well. It is often used for competition free-flight aircraft.

(c) Heavier than the top two wings, the sheet balsa-covered upper leading edge helps to maintain an accurate airfoil section, without the tissue sag between the ribs of the others. An improved type has a sheet-covered front lower surface and vertical balsa webs between the spars, forming a D-box for maximum strength.

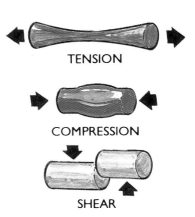

THE WEAKEST LINK

A major weakness is the point at which parts are joined together. These areas often need reinforcing with capping strips and gussets. Glass cloths are also used. In some cases where the structure needs to be small, for example a thin wing section or fuselage, wood is not sufficient and composite materials or even metal are used.

MATERIALS

Different materials have *strength* and *stiffness* in differing amounts. Strength is the ability to resist an applied load without breaking. If pulled a piece of cotton will break quite easily, but not a piece of metal of the same cross-section. Stiffness is the ability to resist deformation when a load is applied. A material with low stiffness is rubber which stretches to great lengths when pulled, but a piece of wire will hardly stretch at all, even when pulled very hard.

Both these general properties can be divided into three major components: *tension* is a force pulling on the material; *compression* is a force pushing on a material; *shear* is a force trying to tear a material in two. So tensile strength

TENSION

COMPRESSION

SHEAR

is the ability of a material to resist a pulling load without breaking, and compression stiffness is its resistance to deformation when a pushing load is applied.

Model aircraft need strength to resist flight and landing loads without breaking, and stiffness to prevent bending and twisting. For best performance, the weight needs to be low, so materials should give just enough strength and stiffness for the lowest weight. We must also consider their density, which is the weight of the material for a given volume. Lead has a high density and balsa a low one.

KEEPING IT TOGETHER

Early model aircraft were made from woods like spruce, pine and bamboo. In the early 1920s, balsa wood was found to have a low density; this transformed models as they could now be made lighter and hence perform better. Recently, composite materials, offering high strength and stiffness with a low density, again allow thinner wing sections to be used in stronger models, improving performance.

WOOD IS GOOD

Balsa is a fast-growing tree, and by felling at different times the wood can have densities between 4 and 24 lb/ft³ (0.06–0.36 gm/cm³). Strength and stiffness is related to density; the lowest density wood will be light and soft, but have a lower strength than the harder and heavier high density wood. Planks of wood cut from the tree in different directions, result in different grains. Balsa is often cut as straight, or A grain, and quarter, or C grain. Straight-grain sheets will bend easily across the grain, but quarter-grain wood will not – an advantage for some model structures. Where high strength and stiffness is needed – in the spars of a highly-loaded wing or fuselage longerons – balsa is not suitable.

Spruce is a harder wood than balsa, has fibres that are closer together and is darker in colour. Strength and stiffness are much better than the

The human-powered Bionic Bat aircraft, designed by former US indoor model-flying champion Dr Paul MacCready, uses a tubular carbon-fibre wing mainspar to resist bending and twisting loads, and carbon cap strips on the foam polystyrene ribs to maintain their shape. Carbon gives high strength for a low weight penalty

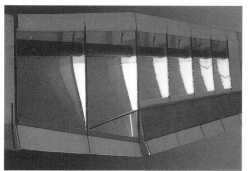

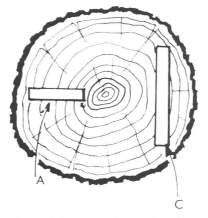

C-cut wood shows quarter grain, stiff across its width, while planks cut in direction A are straight-grained and can be easily rolled into a tube, but are stiffer along their length.

Upper balsa sheet is straight-grained A cut; lower is speckled quarter grain or C-cut wood, used for ribs and resistant to bending across its width.

densest balsa, but as its density is 28 lb/ft³ (0.42 gm/cm³) it should be used only where needed.

Birch plywood is made from a number of thin layers, or laminations, of wood glued together under high pressure. Plywood is made in a range of thicknesses from 0.4 mm to over 12 mm and has a density of 40 lb/ft³ (0.6 gm/cm³). Thus it is used only for highly stressed areas such as root ribs, spar webs and fuselage skinning.

All woods are badly affected by heat and moisture. While strong and stiff for their weight, they can be used only where there is sufficient space, in a thick wing for example. For areas where loads are high and space is small, a different type of material is used.

STRONGER BUT LIGHTER

A **composite** is made from two or more different materials which in themselves may be weak, but when combined produce a much better material. Wood is a natural com-

posite, as it consists of cellulose fibres bound together by lignin in a cellular structure. Balsa wood has very thin cell walls resulting in 40 per cent of the volume containing just air! Hence it has a low density.

Modern composite materials consist of fibres of **carbon**, **Kevlar**, **boron** or **glass** and a glue, or resin, to bind the fibres together. The fibre types have different properties and are available in different forms. **Tows** consist of a large number of very thin fibres bundled together, **unidirectional** material consists of a thin sheet of constant thickness in which the fibres run in the same direction, and **cloth** consists of small bundles of fibres woven together. Composites can also be found as a **mat**, i.e. a short, randomly-oriented thin sheet of material, but this has few applications in model aircraft.

Tows and unidirectional composites are used where the load is in the line of the fibres, i.e. in simple tension or compression. When a shear load is applied, cloths are used and are best when laid at 45°, as individual fibres react the tension and compression loads. Where complex shapes are required, such as fuselage shells, cloths are useful as they will form, or drape, easily into the required shape. Once the resin is applied and has dried, or cured, the shell will be rigid and strong.

The resin is denser than the fibre and will not add to strength and stiffness above a certain percentage of the overall composite, so care must be taken to use as little resin as possible. The fibre usually forms 60 per cent or more of the material.

Different fibres have different properties and this is also true when used in a composite. Kevlar composite has the lowest density but is poor under compression. Carbon has high strength and stiffness in both tension and compression but has a higher density. It is also worse in impact compared to Kevlar, and the cloths available are heavier, limiting their use. Glass has the lowest strength and stiffness and is denser than both carbon and Kevlar, but is available in very light cloths

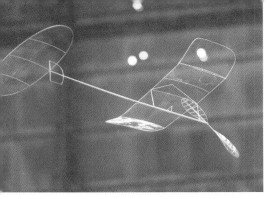

Thinnest of all coverings is microfilm, used on F1D indoor duration aircraft. Variation in the formula results in different thickness; propellers are covered with a thicker film than tailplanes.

and is cheap. Boron has the highest density but is strong and stiff in compression, so is used in applications requiring these properties, like stiffening the leading and trailing edges of indoor microfilm aircraft.

Model aircraft materials need to be strong and stiff but must have low density, so materials are ranked on their strength-to-weight ratio or stiffness-to-weight ratio. Carbon composite is now widely used as these two properties are better than most other materials. This is why carbon composite is commonly used on high-performance full-sized aircraft, Formula One cars and the revolutionary bike that did so well at the 1992 Olympics.

Foam plastics have a very low density, of the order of 2lb/ft³ (0.03 g/cm³), but they have low strength and stiffness and are suitable for small models where the flight loads are very light. Foams are helpful in high-performance model aircraft, too. Buckling occurs when a part doesn't break, but distorts so that it cannot carry much more load. Foam can help by supporting the load-carrying part so it resists this buckling. Typical constructions are wings where a foam plastic core is covered in either thin wood veneer, composite cloth or even aluminium foil. The result is far stronger and stiffer than either the foam alone or the skin alone.

KEEPING OUT THE AIR

Tissue paper, tightened by doping with a cellulose lacquer, provides the overall shape of a wing surface, and also makes the whole wing far more resistant to twisting. Try this with the wing of the rubber model you may build, like the Ajax we describe on pages 72–79.

Early model aircraft were covered in oiled silk, later superseded by doped tissue. Now with modern shrinkable **plastic films**, covering can be quicker and less messy. Various plastic films are available, from those used on tailplanes, which are 0.0025 mm thick and often coated with an aluminium film a few atoms thick for visibility, to films 0.025 mm thick used for wings of free-flight and radio-controlled models. All but the thinnest films are waterproof and lighter than doped tissue but cannot be shrunk as tightly. Thus they can be used only on a structure that doesn't need to be torsionally stiff or which has an underlying structure which is stiff enough without the covering. The thinnest film is the microfilm used on indoor models – only 0.00005 mm thick!

Tissue covering adds torsional stiffness to wooden structures. Most types are quite porous when applied, but several coats of thinned clear dope fill the pores and make the tissue drum-tight and water-resistant. Licence numbers or decoration can be cut from coloured tissue for minimum weight penalty. This is British team member Gary Madelin's FIA glider

described on pages 72–79.

ADHESIVES AND DOPES

Balsa cement is a cellulose acetate or butyrate-based glue that sets by evaporation. Normal cement will dry in about 15 minutes. Some faster-setting cements are useful for field repairs. In general, the longer the drying time, the stronger the joint. For maximum strength, pre-cement the two surfaces with a thin coat of glue rubbed into the wood. Use another coat finally to cement the pieces together. Balsa cement becomes brittle and shrinks with age, distorting badly-fitted joints.

Woodworkers' white glue soaks well into wood, but takes at least an hour to dry. It is not fully waterproof, but does not cause distortion on drying. A doped finish will normally prevent moisture penetrating to the joints.

Epoxy resins are two-part glues that set by chemical action when mixed. Used on clean surfaces they give a strong joint. They can be used to glue metals as well as wood, and many full-sized aircraft have components bonded with this type of glue. Setting times depend on temperature, but fast types are hard within about 30 minutes, while the slower, stronger epoxies take about a day at room temperature.

'Super glues' (cyano-acrylates) depend on an absence of air and the presence of moisture to set, so joints must be accurate, as well as clean. A very small quantity is needed, and an accelerator spray may be used on stubborn joints to initiate the reaction. 'Cyano' also sticks skin fast, and was originally developed as an emergency wound suture for the US forces in Vietnam. Be careful not to get it near eyes; sometimes the fumes produced when it sets can cause asthma-like symptoms. If fingers do get stuck together soak them in warm soapy water, then gently peel, rather than pull, them apart.

Dope is a cellulose acetate-, nitrate- or butyrate-based lacquer used to tighten or waterproof the covering and structure of model aircraft, or to stick the covering to the structure. Use only clear dopes; coloured ones do not tighten and are heavier. Both shrinking and non-shrinking dopes can be bought; the latter may be labelled 'banana oil'. Most need thinning by 50 per cent or more. Use only compatible cellulose thinners. Some people add a small amount of plasticiser to dope to prevent it warping delicate parts.

RUBBER – A GREEN POWER PLANT

The rubber used for flying models is a natural product, so avoid the pale cream-coloured material which is a synthetic butyl-based strip and quite unsuitable.

The property of rubber that interests us is its energy-storage capacity. Energy is put into it by winding and the motor releases it via the propeller. Good rubber (1978 Pirelli is regarded by model flyers as if it was a rare vintage wine) can store about 3,700 feet/pounds per pound (1,110 m kg per kg). In other words, a 4-ounce rubber motor, used in an 'Open' class rubber model, can lift an average 6-foot man his own height.

Raw rubber varies in quality and serious flyers test every batch they buy and save the best for vital competition flights. A simple torque tester can be made as shown.

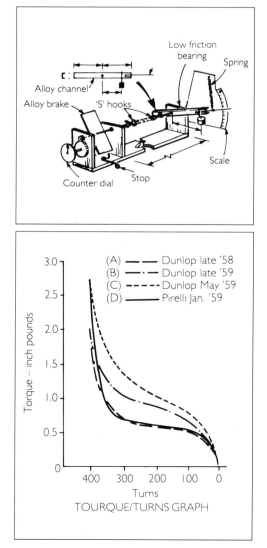

Plotting a graph of turns against torque gives a curve that is S-shaped. The area under the curve indicates the energy-storage capacity of the rubber under test.

Pirelli no longer makes rubber for our purposes, but there are several good mail-order suppliers (see page 96) who do understand free-flight needs. Currently, FAI Supplies in the USA make a tan-coloured rubber that is used by most competition flyers, Champion produce a useful grey rubber and there is some good Chinese rubber, too.

Most rubber is about ¼ inch (1 mm) thick, but several widths are available, and indoor flyers may strip their own to the size they need. Some classes of model have rules limiting rubber weight. A single loop arranged in perhaps 12 or 16 strands is typical for outdoor aircraft. Today motors are made to a length that ensures they are tight between propeller and rear peg; earlier motors were braided to that length or had a system that stopped the propeller before the motor went fully slack.

Turning a large diameter propeller with a coarse pitch requires more twisting force, or torque, than turning a small one. Taking motors of the same weight, a long thin one gives less torque than a short thick one. It takes more turns, though, and will take longer to unwind. Adjust the number of strands in the motor to give the cross-section of rubber needed.

'Breaking-in' a motor before fully winding it is essential. Some stretch the motor to four or five times its slack length and hold it there for perhaps 10 minutes. Others wind to 60, 70, 80 and 90 per cent of maximum turns. The graph shows the maximum turns per inch of motor length.

Winding a small model like the Dart by hand is possible, but it is easier to use a winder. A plastic-geared winder can be bought, or you can make one with Meccano or similar gears. Larger models need a specially-built metal-geared winder or you can adapt a hand-drill.

Stretching the motor to about six times its normal length while winding allows more turns to be

Doug Rowsell of Canada, bronze medallist at the 1991 World Championships, finishes stretch winding his Wakefield. The model is held in a 'stooge', and the metal rod gripped in Doug's teeth is to hold the tightly wound rubber while the propeller is attached.

achieved; when you reach about three-quarters of the intended turns, move in to the model, aiming to complete winding when you reach it. However, a broken motor when winding with the rubber attached to the propeller can destroy both the propeller and the fuselage. Using the winding tube system shown on page 33 prevents this.

A vital item for rubber flying is lubricant. Any mineral oil will soon destroy rubber. Model flyers use mixtures of soft soap, glycerine, surgical jelly or castor oil. Specialist suppliers sell pre-mixed rubber lube. Another rubber-wrecker is ultra-violet light, so keep rubber in the dark or at least shaded. Store it somewhere cool.

The heart of a modern Wakefield. William Beales' uses 14 strands of American-made FAI Supplies tan rubber, turning a glass-cloth covered, carbon-fibre reinforced balsa twin-bladed folding propeller. The shaft runs in twin ball bearings held in a machined duralumin nose assembly, with a snap-on polythene spinner protecting the torque-sensing Montreal stop.

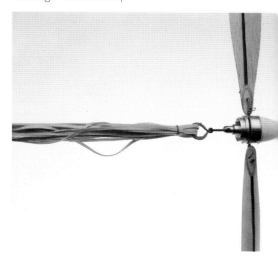

PROPELLERS

Just like a woodscrew, a propeller, or airscrew, has pitch as well as diameter. Pitch is the theoretical distance it would move forwards in one revolution. It is rather like the gear ratio in a car; too coarse a pitch is equivalent to trying to start off in too high a gear – no acceleration. An over-fine pitch will give plenty of acceleration but the rubber motor will run down quickly and the climb will suffer. Of course, you need enough weight of rubber to fly the model; you wouldn't find a hedge-trimmer motor in a Formula 1 car.

The Darts included with this book have simple moulded plastic propellers, but when the rubber power ends the propeller can freewheel. This reduces the drag and thus improves the glide. Most competition aircraft used this system till the late 1930s. When Dick Korda won the Wakefield World Championships using a folding-blade propeller, and a single blade at that, flyers saw this as the way to improve the glide further.

The single-bladed propeller was thought by some to be more efficient than a two-blader, as it was operating in less disturbed air; a counterbalance weight was fitted on the opposite side. Later on came two-bladed folders, which are the norm today.

To ensure that the blade or blades fold in the same position on every flight, some sort of mechanical stop is needed. A compression spring opposes the tension of the rubber motor, so as the motor unwinds the propeller moves forwards till an arm on the propeller shaft engages the stop on the rear of the noseblock, allowing the blades to be folded back by the airflow.

Improvements are still possible. Rubber varies slightly in thickness and considerably in its torque characteristics. Relying on the reducing tension of the motor to stop the propeller sometimes produces random bunches of part-wound rubber and these move the centre of gravity of the aircraft and upset the glide. Wakefield flyers in the Montreal area came up with a system that senses the drop in torque, rather than tension, to stop the propeller. The Montreal stop, often with variations like a variable pitch device and a means of locking the blades into the 'feathered' or minimum drag position for launch, is now almost universal for world championships

Above left Terry Dilks' 24-inch (600 mm) twin-bladed folding propeller is for an Open Class model used in domestic British contests. It uses a spring-loaded clutch that disengages as the rubber torque drops, allowing a pin to pop into a locating hole on the front of the noseblock and lock the propeller before it folds.

Above centre Nineteen-inch (500 mm) single-bladed folding propeller for Dick Korda's 1939 Wakefield Cup winner, shown on pages 38/39; a lead counterbalance weight prevents vibration. The spring-loaded shaft slides forward in the propeller hub as the rubber tension drops, allowing an arm on the shaft to engage a screw on the rear of the noseblock and stop the propeller so it folds along the fuselage side.

Above right Eighteen-inch (460 mm) diameter freewheeling propeller for Bob Copland's 1946 Wakefield, shown on pages 34/35, is carved from a single block of balsa. The spinner houses the clutch for the freewheel mechanism.

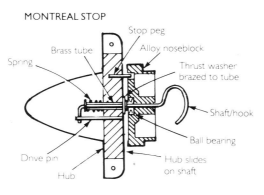

MONTREAL STOP

Stop peg · Brass tube · Alloy noseblock · Spring · Thrust washer brazed to tube · Shaft/hook · Ball bearing · Drive pin · Hub slides on shaft · Hub

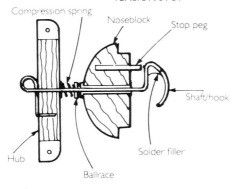

TENSION STOP

Compression spring · Noseblock · Stop peg · Shaft/hook · Hub · Solder filler · Ballrace

Roger Ruppert moulded the folding blades for his 1991 Wakefield's 26 inch (660 mm) propeller from carbon cloth with a foam plastic core. This gives a stiff blade that transmits the rubber power efficiently. The anodised aluminium alloy hub contains the torque-sensing Montreal stop.

THE CRAZY RUBBER BAND

This short discussion of the preparation, treatment and (ab)use of rubber motors may encourage you to join the Crazy Rubber Band in pursuit of aerodynamic perfection.

Today's Wakefields are allowed only 1.4 ounce (40 g) motors, normally tight in the fuselage, but a vintage motor may be around 4 ounces (110 g) and must be pre-tensioned, or braided, to ensure it distributes itself evenly after unwinding. One way, when making up a 12-strand motor, is to produce two 6-strand loops, joined with a bobbin fixed to a secure anchor; wind half the tensioning turns clockwise on to each half, and then bring the two free ends together on the motor hook. Then lightly wind the 12 strands and let them unwind again, producing a neatly-braided motor.

To get full power and efficiency from a rubber motor, winding to maximum turns needs a keen appreciation of the forces involved, strong equipment, attention to detail and a total lack of fear. Models are held in a winding jig or 'stooge', secured to the ground by guy-ropes. A rod, passed through a hollow rear motor

This specially-made winder (top), made by David Stapleton for Free-Flight News Supplies, uses twin ball bearings and a turns counter, as well as a pistol grip for safety and a spring-loaded locking hook to attach the S-hook of the rubber motor. Gear ratio is 4:1. It is suitable for the most powerful motors. Beneath is a light duty commercial plastic winder for indoor models or the Delta Dart. Ratio is 10:1.

Ramon Alban with the rubber motor of his Zombie V of the late 1940s at full stretch. The model is in a winding 'stooge' for one-person operation. The propeller is ready on the ground; it will be attached when the motor is fully wound and the winding tube inside the fuselage for protection is slid out.

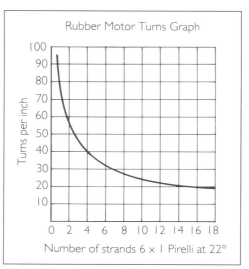

Rubber Motor Turns Graph

(Graph: Turns per inch (y-axis, 10 to 100) vs Number of strands 6 × 1 Pirelli at 22° (x-axis, 0 to 18))

peg, holds the fuselage, with a jig extension supporting its front end. The tube-winding system avoids damage if a motor breaks, and often a torque meter is used to check the energy stored in the motor, with a mechanical turns counter on the winder. The winder may be a modified hand-drill, with the chuck removed and the shaft drilled to take a stout wire winding hook.

The turns graph shows the likely maximum a motor will take; for a 46-inch (1,170 m) 14-strand motor of FAI Tan rubber this will be about 920 turns. The 80+ ounce/inches of torque that results is a key factor in the climb performance. If you launch with more torque than you have trimmed for, the model may loop or power stall.

Zero the counter, and gently take up the slack by winding on a few turns as you walk backwards from the model in its 'stooge'. After about 50 turns the motor should be stretched to three or four times its normal length, and for that 46-inch motor the winder is about 16–20 feet (5–6 m) from the nose of the model. Notice that any spectators will have taken a couple of involuntary steps back from the proceedings in a nervous gesture of self-preservation. This luxury is denied to the model flyer, who stays directly aligned with the whole shebang for the next few minutes, and whose lips may be seen moving as he utters a quiet prayer. When about half the target turns are reached, he winds on the rest as he walks slowly in towards the aeroplane, occasionally checking the torque meter, and judging the arrival of the motor hook at the model nose as he winds on the last few turns.

Deep breathing usually takes place here, before the protective winding tube is slid out of the fuselage to expose the motor hook again just outside the nose. A short steel rod is slid through the motor hook and the flyer firmly grasps this and the motor, before freeing the extension winding rod and replacing it with the propeller. Engaging the free-wheel clutch or the Montreal stop, and the propeller lock if the Wakefield is a current type, ensures that all those turns do not run off at once in a spectacular and totally destructive shaft run. Removing the rod holding the rear peg to the 'stooge' frees the model.

Vintage Wakefields had no propeller lock, so all the torque had to be held by hand till the model was launched. It takes both hands to steady the aircraft, and to minimise the risk of wind damage. A final check of wing, tail and fin, maybe the multi-function timer (vintage models don't have this mixed bless-

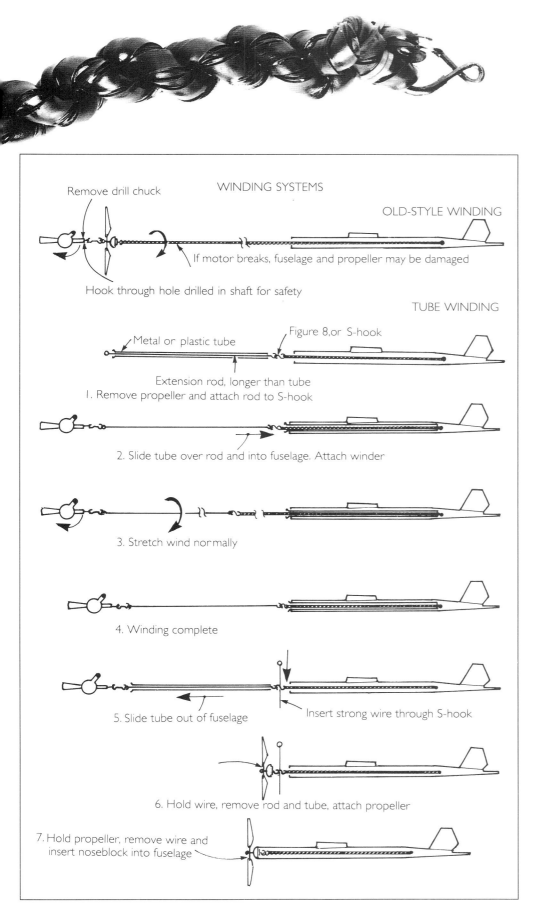

WINDING SYSTEMS

OLD-STYLE WINDING

Remove drill chuck

If motor breaks, fuselage and propeller may be damaged

Hook through hole drilled in shaft for safety

TUBE WINDING

Metal or plastic tube

Figure 8, or S-hook

Extension rod, longer than tube

1. Remove propeller and attach rod to S-hook

2. Slide tube over rod and into fuselage. Attach winder

3. Stretch wind normally

4. Winding complete

5. Slide tube out of fuselage

Insert strong wire through S-hook

6. Hold wire, remove rod and tube, attach propeller

7. Hold propeller, remove wire and insert noseblock into fuselage

This motor is for an Open Rubber class model flown by British national champion Russell Peers. It weighs 3¾ ounces (107 g) and is braided to prevent bunching when fully unwound in the model.

hard and almost vertically; for a heart-stopping second nothing happens. Then as the momentum of the throw decays, the propeller starts and the model hurtles up, to join the other one, screaming silently in a right-hand spiral. The climb angles reduce; the propeller blades of the fast-climbing modern model fold after 40 seconds, but the vintage Wakefield, with almost triple the rubber weight, climbs for twice as long until it is a dot in the sky. The older model's 18-inch (460 mm) propeller freewheels, with blades big enough to hide a baby's arms, and it soars like a buzzard, wings outstretched in the warm rising air where the modern Wakefield soon joins it.

But trickery is at hand. Fuse-burned rubber bands and timers powered by a child's converted clockwork toy pop the dethermalisers. The soaring man-made buzzards are reduced to aerodynamic enigmas, their lift killed; instead of falling like a bag of hammers, they slowly spiral down through the rising air finally to land again safely, ready for more competition flights.

Sixteen-year-old Wakefield flyer Arkadiusz Kudla competed on the Polish team at the 1988 World Junior Free-Flight Championships at Leszno, Poland.

ing), set the dethermaliser, walk to the launch area, sense the breeze and feel for a puff of warmer air that signals a passing thermal.

Now the vintage flyer makes a special obeisance to the weather gods; he bends the knee to touch the wheels and the under-fin on the tarmac. He releases the propeller micro-seconds before letting go of the fuselage, without the push that

the rules ban, facing the breeze as the model is freed.

His modern Wakefield-flying equivalent, limited for motor weight but unlimited for ingenious systems to wring height from it, uses the muscle power that his vintage colleague must shun, as well as a carefully programmed timer to optimise the climb. Spotting the same thermal, he hand-launches his aircraft

COPLAND'S WAKEFIELD

Bob Copland's constant quest for efficiency culminated in his 1946 Wakefield. Regarded by many as the ultimate in vintage rubber models, its circular section fuselage, with a spinner to minimise the drag of the propeller hub, and carefully faired fillets at the roots of the plug-in shoulder wings, all helped to give it a good climb and a flat glide.

This modern replica was built by Peter Lee. The wingspan is 46 inches (1,170 mm), and the freewheeling propeller is 18 inches (460 mm) in diameter. The power is 12 strands of $\frac{1}{4} \times \frac{1}{4}$ inch (6 x 1 mm) rubber. Total weight is 8¼ ounces (210 g). Building the streamlined fuselage, with its many $\frac{1}{16}$ inch (1.5 mm) square stringers, was regarded as one of the major building challenges of the period.

Fourteen-year-old Alan Hardwick with Peter Lee's replica of Bob Copland's 1946 streamlined Wakefield, designed to the old rules that required a minimum fuselage cross section of length²/100.

Cover of *Aeromodeller* magazine for August 1951 shows Bob Copland in action at a contest, with the perfect push-free rise-off-ground launch for his classic streamlined Wakefield. Plans of this aircraft are still available from Aeromodeller Plans Service.

Bob Copland designed the Hawker Hurricane 2D's bulletproof windscreen and the external rearview mirror, here visible above and in front of the pilot's head. The aircraft was fitted with a pair of 40 mm cannon for anti-tank work during the Second World War.

COPLAND

Bob Copland's imagination was caught by model aircraft at the age of 18 when he and a friend bought some old copies of the American *Air Trails* magazine in a market in London's Farringdon Road. Drawings and articles on hand-launched gliders and indoor flying models led them to build a rubber-powered microfilm-covered aircraft and enter a competition at Alexandra Palace. The current British indoor duration record was about four minutes and, much to his surprise, Bob more than doubled it.

Recruited into the Northern Heights club by C.A. Rippon (founder of the Ripmax concern), Bob, who was training to be a chartered accountant, then won a place on the British team competing for the Wakefield Trophy in the USA in 1936. Two years later he flew in the King Peter Cup event in Yugoslavia. On Bob's return, he was introduced to Sidney Camm, chief designer at Hawker Aircraft, who invited him to join the company as a draughtsman. Bob's talent at this had been developed via his model flying interest.

Bob's first job at Hawker was to design the bulletproof windscreen for the then-new Hurricane fighter. This he followed with the simple-sounding rearview mirror, which he designed to be mounted externally, to improve the pilot's view of pursuing German fighters. Camm disapproved of this excrescence on his clean-lined aircraft, but the addition actually improved the turbulent airflow over the Hurricane's steep windscreen and added 5 mph (8 km/hr) to the top speed. Later,

Bob Copland, who continued to fly Wakefields competitively until well after the war, worked on the Typhoon, Tempest, Sea Hawk and in fact every aircraft the company produced. When he retired from British Aerospace, which had absorbed Hawker years before, he was chief design engineer, with responsibility for the Hawk and the Sea Harrier.

The aircraft that he flew in Yugoslavia was the GB 3, and it played a major part in the British team win, just a year before the outbreak of the Second World War, which devastated the country. Unlike most of its foreign competitors, GB 3 had a superbly streamlined fuselage and a shoulder-mounted wing to reduce drag to a minimum. Bob used a large freewheeling propeller, carved from a single block of balsa and with a spinner to enclose its freewheeling mechanism.

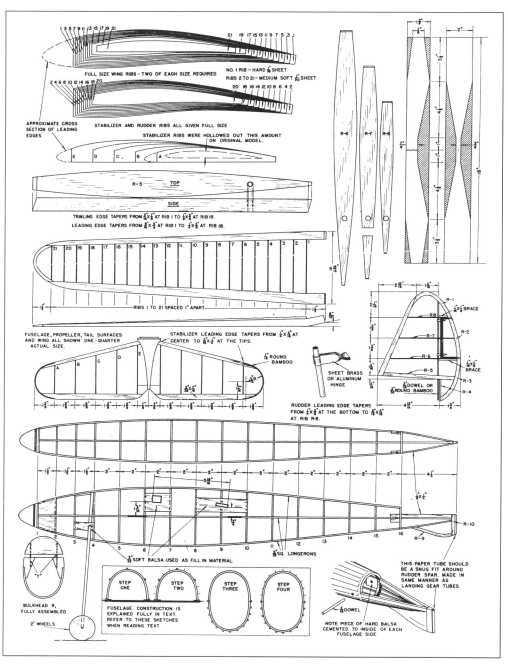

The contest, on a large airfield near Ljubljana in Slovenia, took place in almost no wind, with blue skies and temperatures around 30 degrees. Bob had already that year set a British record of almost 28 minutes with GB 3 at Fairey's aerodrome, now the site of Heathrow airport. On day two of the Yugoslav contest, after undistinguished times on the previous day, Bob launched his model from the take-off boards. The 3-ounce (85 g) rubber motor gave a fast long climb of about 90 seconds. As the propeller began to freewheel, GB 3 met a thermal that started to build steadily; two large army range-finders were tracking the model and a maximum height of over 9,000 feet (2,800 m) was recorded. The model finally landed

ing excess drag and upsetting the trim of the model so it descended in a steep nose-down attitude.

Building a Copland Wakefield fuselage is not easy. The circular formers are wound from laminations of ⅟₃₂-inch (0.8 mm) balsa strip round cardboard templates. There are 15 of them, all of different diameters. Each template has a square hole in its exact centre to locate it on a square rod. The ⅟₁₆ inch (1.5 mm) square balsa stringers, 24 of them, are then carefully cemented into place on the formers and lined up to be absolutely straight. The rod is then removed and the templates slid out of each former, leaving the completed fuselage ready to cover. Easier said than done, but Bob Copland was a meticulous builder.

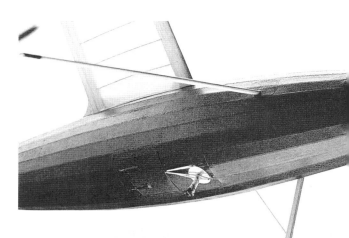

A slow-burning fuse melted through a rubber band, holding closed a trapdoor under the fuselage of Bob Copland's Wakefield. When the door popped open at the end of the required flight time, a parachute came out, attached to the tail of the aircraft. This early form of dethermaliser increased the drag and brought the aircraft down in a steep glide. The drawing below shows the operation.

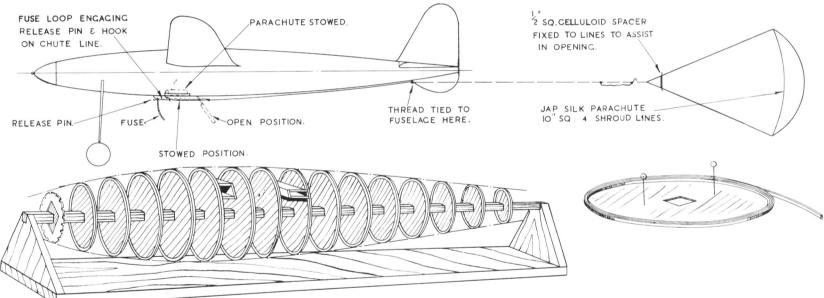

after 33 minutes 9 seconds, having drifted only three-quarters of a mile (1,200 m).

After the war, Bob flew the model on pages 34–35. This was an improvement on GB 3, with a more efficient higher aspect ratio wing, using the new Davis airfoil instead of the RAF 32 that GB 3 employed. The wing of the B-24 Liberator bomber used a similar airfoil.

Another innovation was to use a dethermaliser to bring the model down for further flights. For this Bob chose a parachute stowed inside the fuselage until a slow-burning fuse opened the trapdoor enclosing it. The 'chute, attached to the rear of the fuselage, then opened, produc-

Left The plan of Bob Copland's GB3 Wakefield, winner of the King Peter Cup in Yugoslavia in 1938, appeared in a 1940 issue of the now-vanished US magazine *Air Trails*, shortly before the Battle of Britain . The fuselage was an oval section, rather than circular as on his post-war models. The upper half was built first, with the formers cut from two laminated cross-grained balsa sheets, and the small-section balsa stringers cemented to them. This half was then removed from the building board and the second half built on to it.

On Bob's post-war Wakefields (above) fuselage formers were laminated from a thin strip of balsa, wound in two layers round a false circular former of cardboard, waxed to prevent them sticking to it. The 15 formers on their false cores were then mounted on a square rod held at each end on a jig. The 24 ⅟₁₆ inch (1.5 mm) square balsa stringers were then glued in place before the rod was slid out and the false formers removed.

Bob Copland was chief design engineer for the vertical take-off British Aerospace Harrier, the final aircraft with which he worked during his long career in model and full-size aviation.

WAKEFIELD WINNER

US team member Dick Korda's Wakefield Cup win in the United States a month before the outbreak of war in 1939 set a record of 43 minutes 29 seconds, thanks to a long-lasting thermal of rising air. As a result the idea of a maximum duration for each flight was introduced after the war, to reduce the effect of a single long flight, along with a limit on rubber motor weight.

The Korda Wakefield typified the classic slab-sided duration model, and was kitted by at least three different manufacturers in the USA and Britain. The single-bladed propeller folds neatly along the fuselage side at the end of the power run to reduce the drag and improve the glide. Almost half the total weight of 8¼ ounces (210 g) is the rubber motor.

This Korda replica was built by John Meaney of Great Britain, over 50 years after the model's Wakefield Cup success. When he is not flying vintage model aircraft, John is a flight engineer on Boeing 747s.

Californian flyer Jim Persson launches his pre-war rules 4 ounce (110 g) Chet Lanzo Wakefield at an international contest at the School of Army Flying at Middle Wallop.

Arne Ellila of Finland won the Wakefield Cup in 1949 and 1950 with this design. Here Pecorani of Italy releases his example for a smooth take-off at a 1990 contest.

The late Butch Hadland, one of Britain's most respected indoor scale-flyers, in action in 1991 with a Bob Copland 1936 Wakefield, built to the 4-ounce rules.

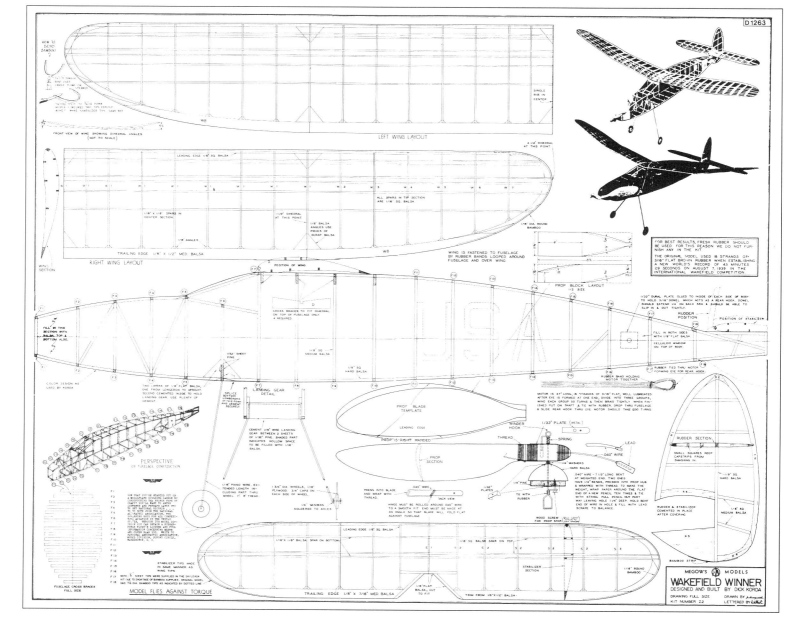

The structure of Dick Korda's 1939 Wakefield was similar to many of its competitors. Rubber bands holding the wing to the top of the fuselage reduce the risk of damage by letting it skew on impact. The single-bladed propeller was quicker to make and also avoided problems of carving two identical blades. When folded along the fuselage side it also avoided the risk of breakage common to freewheeling types.

The wing used several small section spars, which improved the lift by turbulating the airflow and delaying the stall.

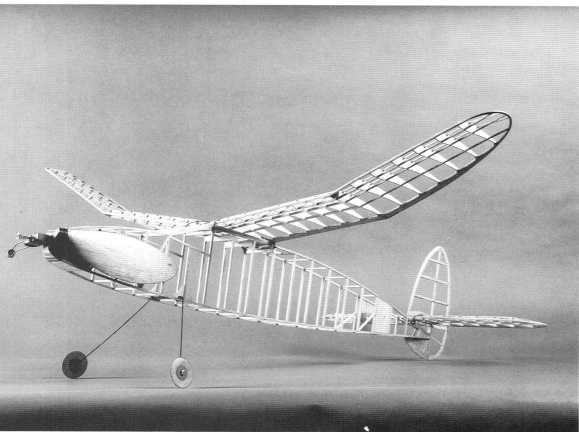

OUTDOOR FREE FLIGHT TODAY

Since the mid-1970s there has been a revival of interest in vintage models like the Copland and Korda Wakefields. First in the USA, and then in Britain and elsewhere, the Society of Antique Modelers (a misnomer, really: it's the models, not the flyers, that are of old design) formed chapters to encourage the flying of replicas of pre-1951 models. But free-flight is as modern as tomorrow, too, and for many people flying high-performance duration aircraft is a fascinating challenge.

World championships are held for them as they are for radio-controlled and control-line model flying. Club, local and national contests are organised, too. Don't make the mistake, though, of seeing radio-flying as the pinnacle; all three disciplines are an intriguing blend of man-and-machine plus man-versus-the-elements.

As well as being the oldest class, outdoor free-flight also attracts the largest entry today; often 35 nations compete at its World Championships, held in the odd-numbered years. (They alternate with the European Championships.) Teams consist of nine people, three of whom fly gliders, three fly rubber-powered aircraft and three fly engine-assisted gliders. Recent winners have come from China, Russia, France, Hungary, the USA and Israel. A new addition is a championships for under-18s.

The free-flight community is international and very friendly. Language differences vanish as flyers share techniques and discuss solutions to the universal challenges of designing a more efficient aircraft and keeping it in the air for longer. The shared problems are solved by ingenuity and determination, and each flight is unique. The sport is creative, clean and competitive, but the competing is as much with the elements and yourself as with the other flyers.

Today's international rules limit things like the weight of rubber motor allowed, the maximum wing area, the minimum weight, the engine capacity or, for gliders, the towline length. These all limit the flight duration of the aircraft, and make it vital to launch into helpful rising air, the secret of a long flight. Today you do not have to build your own model for most classes, but many people still find designing and building an original aircraft that is stiffer or stronger for the same weight, or uses the rubber or engine power to climb higher or glide longer, adds interest.

WAKEFIELD TROPHY WINNERS			
Date	Winner	Nation	Venue
1928	T. Newell	GB	GB
1929	R. Bullock	GB	GB
1930	J. Earhardt	USA	GB
1931	J. Earhardt	USA	USA
1932	G. Light	USA	USA
1933	J. Kenworthy	GB	GB
1934	J. Allman	GB	GB
1935	G. Light	USA	GB
1936	A. Judge	GB	USA
1937	E. Fillon	France	GB
1938	J. Cahill	USA	France
1939	R. Korda	USA	USA
1948	R. Chesterton	GB	USA
1949	A. Ellila	Finland	GB
1950	A. Ellila	Finland	Finland
1951	S. Stark	Sweden	Finland
1952	A. Blomgren	Sweden	Sweden
1953	J. Foster	USA	GB
1954	A. King	Australia	USA
1955	G. Samann	W. Germany	W.Germany
1956	L. Petersen	Sweden	Sweden
1958	R. Baker	Australia	GB
1959	F. Dvořak	Czechoslovakia	France
1961	G. Reich	USA	W.Germany
1963	J. Löffler	E. Germany	Austria
1965	T. Köster	Denmark	Finland
1967	M. Sulkala	Finland	Czechoslovakia
1969	A. Oschatz	E. Germany	Austria
1971	J. Klima	Czechoslovakia	Sweden
1973	J. Löffler	E. Germany	Austria
1975	Park Chang Sung	N. Korea	Bulgaria
1977	Kim Dong Sik	N. Korea	Denmark
1979	I. Ben-Itzhak	Israel	USA
1981	L. Döring	W. Germany	Spain
1983	L. Döring	W. Germany	Australia
1985	R. Höfsass	W. Germany	Yugoslavia
1987	R. White	USA	France
1989	E. Cofalik	Poland	Argentina
1991	A. Andrjukov	USSR	Yugoslavia

Top A young New Zealand flyer launches his P-30 class model at the National Championships at Gore, South Island. The zig-zag wing and tail ribs prevent warps.

Above Thirteen-year-old Emil Biber was a Bulgarian Wakefield team member at the World Junior Free-Flight Championships at Leszno, Poland in 1988.

Below British Open Rubber flyer Phil Ball launches his model in the evening calm at the 1985 Club Championships on Salisbury Plain. The flight was a record fly-off time of 25 minutes 29 seconds.

FISHING FOR LIFT

Playing the glider delicately like a trout for a quarter of an hour or more to find the centre of a column of rising air is vital to boost the duration of FlA models. Maximising the time in the air is the sole aim for these delicate-looking yet incredibly strong aircraft, and fitness plays quite a part in the results. The glider is kited into the air at the other end of a 164-foot (50 m) towline. Successful competitors, such as Andres Lepp of Estonia or Mike Fantham of Great Britain, feel for the slight tug of a thermal up-current, lifting the glider as it flies through warm air.

The sight of maybe a dozen or more of these fascinating aircraft, soaring away in lazy silent circles and sharing their thermal with feathered experts like storks or buzzards, is a thrill even to a non-flying spectator.

Left British FIC team member Stafford Screen launches Mike Fantham's Robin FIA glider during the World Championships at Cordoba, Argentina, in 1989. Round his neck hangs a compass, vital for retrieving.

Right A stylish FIA glider launch by an Australian helper at the World Championships in Argentina.

The British three-man FIA glider team at the European Free-Flight Championships at Sibiu, Romania, in 1992. Chris Edge (left) and Mike Fantham (right) are both design engineers from British Aerospace, and John Carter is a former rally driver.

Chris Edge's World Championships F1A glider spans 7 feet 2 inches (2.2 metres), yet weighs only 14⅓ ounces (410 g). It uses a radio location beacon to aid retrieval, and has a moulded carbon-fibre leading edge D-box to resist wing flutter during launch.

WORLD CHAMPIONSHIP GLIDERS

Free-flight gliders are usually towed into the air, rather like a kite, on a 164-foot (50 m) towline; the flyer may need to run into the wind, and the timing of the flight starts when the aircraft releases from the line.

Gliders in the World Championship class (FlA) must weigh at least 14½ ounces (410 g) and have a total wing and tailplane horizontal projected area between 496 and 527 square inches (32–34 dm²). This size of glider originated in Scandinavia in the 1940s, and is also known as the Nordic A/2 type, its original title.

An international class exists for smaller gliders, too. The FAI's class FlH (originally the Nordic A/1) has a maximum horizontal area of 279 square inches (18 dm²) and a minimum weight of 7.76 ounces (220 g).

For towline gliders, as for most competition free-flight aircraft, the sole aim is to maximise the time in the air. It is possible to feel for a thermal up-current while towing the glider, rather like an angler delicately plays a trout. However, it would be helpful to have as much height as possible when the flight starts, just in case the thermal dies away.

Launching the glider faster than its normal gliding speed will certainly help, but is likely to cause a stall as the speed finally drops off with the nose high; this can often result in the glider losing more height than it gained. To avoid this, flyers carefully adjust the wing warps so that the aircraft eases into its normal glide circle as the airspeed drops after a hard launch.

For years, free-flight gliders used a towhook that was essentially an open hook facing to the rear. When you slackened the towline tension, the drag of a pennant at the top end of the line pulled the towline off the hook. It was usual to have an auto-rudder system that held the rudder straight during tow, allowing it to spring over to the glide circle position as the towline released.

A development that originated from the Soviet flyers in the late 1960s locks the model temporarily on to the towline. However, the simple towhook is replaced by a hook that swings back as the line tension is reduced, allowing the rudder to swing over and let the glider circle tightly while still attached to the line. This has several advantages. Now we can test the air by circling in it and seeing whether the model goes up; if not, run off to another patch of air and try again. You can tow the glider downwind of other models and launch when they start to climb in a thermal. Instead of having to run steadily into wind you can even pause to catch your breath,

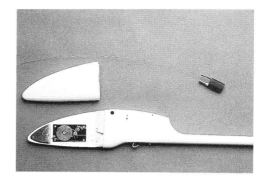

A moulded glass and carbon-fibre shroud on Chris Edge's F1A glider covers the clockwork timer that operates the variable incidence tailplane and the dethermaliser; note the lead nose weight. The radio beacon, shown removed, weighs 0.1 ounces (3 g), including the battery, which is the silver cylinder below the aerial.

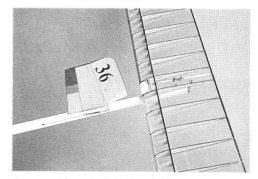

Auto-rudder of Chris Edge's F1A glider shows the line connecting it to the moving towhook. Tailplane has carbon caps to ribs and mainspar and carbon trailing edge; it is covered with Mylar film for lightness.

Launching a world championship glider
A) The glider tows straight and kites up when the towline is tight.
B) The flyer slows up, letting the towline slacken.
C) With a slack towline the rudder moves over and the glider circles tightly, still attached.
D) Running hard accelerates the glider straight to the top of the towline and unlatches the hook.

F1E gliders use a magnet coupled to a rudder at the nose to keep the aircraft pointing into the wind and the lift created when it meets a slope. Here long-time competitor Trevor Faulkner of Great Britain launches at an international contest.

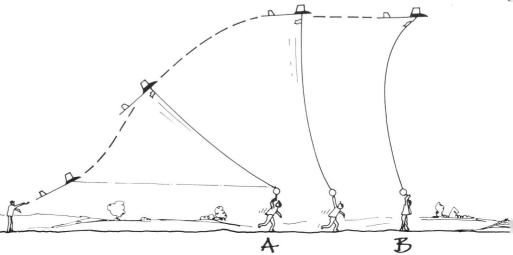

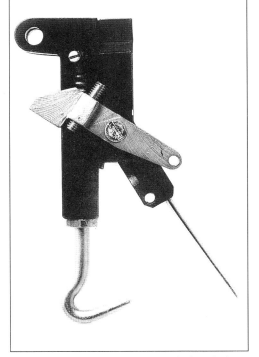

The heart of today's FlA glider is the circle towhook. This Russian one is typical. It is pivoted in the fuselage from the hole at the top. The latch at the lower right, shown open, retains the tow-ring on the hook until a hard pull on the towline extends the hook downwards against a spring, allowing the glider to fly free. A line attaches the lighter-coloured arm to the rudder, pulling it straight when the towline tension is moderately high, and letting it move to a circling position when the towline is slack.

E) The flyer releases the towline with the glider flying very fast. It drops off the hook, and this starts the timer as the model climbs steeply. About a second later the timer pulls the tailplane down at its rear, pitching the nose down sharply towards level flight. A fraction of a second later still, the tailplane returns to normal and the glider circles away, much higher than the towline height. Finally, the timer dethermalises the glider several minutes later.

without seeing the model fall off the slack towline — a big advantage to the less fit. When you are finally sure that your glider is in strong lift, a hard sprint opens the towhook latch and lets the model fly free. At the same time the dethermaliser timer starts.

Another variation on this technique, one that uses the flyer's energy input more effectively, came after Sergei Makarov and Mikhail Kochkarev from Moscow did an extensive computer study of glider launching. They found that a steep, straight ahead climb from a high-speed release could give a useful height gain (often 30 feet/10 m or so) if the timer was also used to pull the tailplane down hard to a positive angle of incidence half a second or so after release, to kill the stall, and then returned to the glide setting. This quarter bunt, called after the aerobatic manoeuvre that causes 'red-out' in pilots, needs some pretty cunning timer technology, but is becoming popular in major contests.

The need to increase launch height puts severe demands on the structure of a glider. The bending strain on the wing at launch is very high, often up to 20G (20 times gravity), which is far more than the latest jet fighter aircraft must withstand. The glider must survive this for flight after flight. This is why many of today's top models use a carbon fibre mainspar and a wing leading edge D-box moulded from Kevlar, the material used for bulletproof flak-jackets.

For the fuselage tailboom, most of today's gliders use a tapered carbon fibre tube, chosen for its stiffness and lightness. These were originally sections of fishing rod, but are now specially produced for free-flight use.

To enjoy free-flight glider-flying it is not essential to resort to composite construction and high technology. Mike Fantham, who designs advanced aircraft structures for a major aerospace company, has had a string of international contest wins using his Robin FlA design. This has a balsa and spruce structure, with glasscloth covering on the wing leading edge to reduce twisting, and a basic circle towhook launch system.

There is another glider class that needs no towline. FlEs are slope soaring gliders but are allowed to use an automatic on-board steering system. This is usually a bar magnet, coupled to a rudder (often a second one, mounted at the nose of the aircraft). The magnet always points north, and can be set so that it moves the rudder to keep the glider heading into the wind blowing on to the slope. This produces a steady slope lift, in which the aircraft soars. Not surprisingly, mountainous nations like Austria and Slovakia do well in FlE.

Li Sung Chol of North Korea, placed second at the first World Junior Free-Flight Championships held at Leszno, Poland, in 1988, flying an FlA glider. He is on the way to a competition flight here, accompanied by an interpreter.

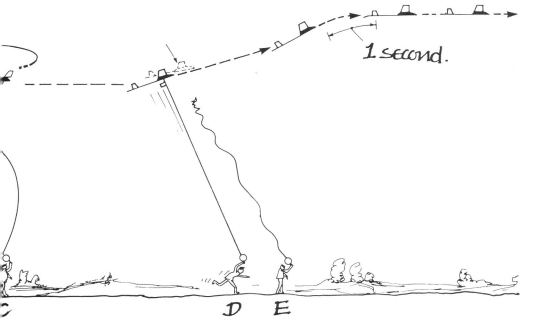

1 second.

RUBBER MAGIC

Flying a rubber model in competition has a special appeal. Part of this appeal is the silence, broken only by the urgent whirr of a fast-turning propeller and the slight whistle of a rapidly-climbing aircraft. Using the earliest form of aircraft motive power, boosted by decades of steady improvement in technique, adds to the thrill. The building excitement, common to all of today's free-flight contests, as flyers wait with fully-wound motors for a thermal and closely watch for the slight changes in wind and temperature that mark its arrival, heightens the drama. Sooner or later someone decides to launch. If the climb looks good and the height suggests thermal assistance, a dozen or more models soon spiral urgently up towards the first, and are soon circling away downwind. Once you try it, you will probably be hooked for life.

This 59-inch (1,500 mm) wingspan FIB Wakefield class rubber-powered aircraft by 1993 British team member William Beales has a motor tube of carbon cloth and Kevlar to withstand motor breakages. The propeller blades are reinforced with carbon fibre and covered with glass cloth.

Far left British National Champion Russell Peers launches his Wakefield during the World Championships at Cordoba, Argentina, in 1989. Fluorescent orange wingtips help to locate the model after it lands.

Left Evgeny Gorbanj of the Soviet Union puts all his energy into the launch of his Wakefield at Zrenjanin, Yugoslavia, during the 1991 World Championships. The propeller blades are locked, and will start turning about half a second later.

Below British Wakefield team member Keith Chamberlain prepares to wind during the 1992 World Junior Championships at Lucenec, Slovakia. The 'stooge' holding the aircraft allows him to wind single-handed.

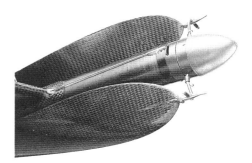

Twin folding propeller blades on Swiss flyer Roger Ruppert's FIB Wakefield are moulded from carbon fibre cloth, as is the fuselage. The blades are locked forwards for launching until the timeswitch lets the motor drive them half a second later.

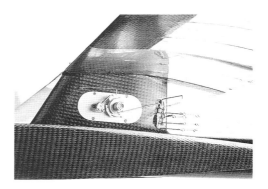

The timer on the side of the pylon operates the propeller start, tailplane incidence, rudder adjuster and dethermaliser. It is made from the converted nylon clockwork drive mechanism of a Tomy toy. The patterning is the weave of the carbon cloth used to mould the pylon and the propeller blades (here folded along the fuselage side).

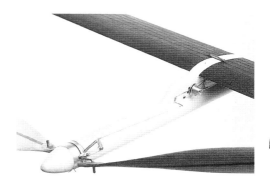

1993 British team member William Beales's Wakefield has a motor tube of carbon cloth and Kevlar to withstand motor breakages. The black lines on the wing are thin graphic tape strips to improve the airflow over the wing and increase the lift. The timer-controlled trigger behind the propeller holds it locked until almost a second after launch.

Propeller blades fold at end of power run, typically at 35 seconds, and glide starts.

Timer alters rudder to glide turn position at about 25 seconds.

Timer returns wing and tailplane to normal incidence at about 6 seconds.

Timer unlocks the propeller less than a second after a hard launch. One wing is now at increased incidence to counter the high initial torque of the rubber. Tailplane incidence is high to counter looping tendency.

WORLD CHAMPIONSHIP RUBBER-POWERED AIRCRAFT

For many years the Wakefield rules included a requirement for models to take-off from the ground, which often led to damage in gusty weather. The fuselage also had to fit a cross section formula (length ^{2}/100), which led to a bulky and weak structure, again prone to damage. There was no limit on rubber motor weight, so fuselages often collapsed under the tension of too much rubber. The models that survived were capable of long flights with help from thermals, but flyers wanted a contest in which luck played a smaller part.

To make the aircraft less damage-prone and to limit the flight duration, a sequence of rule changes were made that allowed hand-launching, removed the fuselage formula and restricted the rubber weight, eventually to today's 1.4 ounces (40 g). First three, then five and finally seven flights were needed as competitions became more challenging and more interesting.

As well as the rubber motor weight limit, today's Wakefields must have a minimum airframe weight of 6.7 ounces (190 g), with a horizontal area from 263 to 294 square inches (17–19 dm²).

Fly-ability

The idea of a maximum duration for each flight made consistency impor-

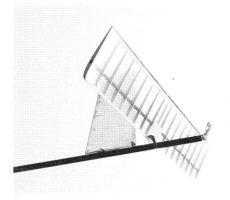

The structure of Swiss Wakefield flyer Roger Ruppert's 1992 aircraft is almost all carbon fibre, permitting a very hard hand launch and a resulting height gain. The wing spans 61 inches (1,564 mm) and the aircraft weighs 8.1 ounces (230 g), including the 1.4-ounce (40 g) rubber motor.

Timer operates dethermaliser, usually after 3-minute 'max' flight.

tant, and having a minimum airframe weight meant that models could be built strong enough to be flown in rough conditions, as well as allowing various mechanisms to be carried to adjust the aircraft in flight.

Muscle + Rubber = Climb

As with gliders, the secret of success with rubber models is to climb as high as possible. To do this, some of today's Wakefields use the dethermaliser timer to trigger a delayed propeller start. This allows the model to be hand-launched very hard, but with the propeller blades locked stationary for about half a second. The rubber motor then starts with the model perhaps 10 to 12 feet (3–4 m) higher than its flyer, and a valuable few seconds longer glide time results. Like modern free-flight gliders, many Wakefields use a carbon and Kevlar structure to prevent the wing from fluttering during the fast launch.

The 1.4-ounce (40 g) motors used today give around 35 seconds' climb, depending on the propeller diameter and pitch. As we saw on page 31, the power output of a rubber motor is not constant through its run, so the timer also adjusts the tailplane incidence and rudder settings during the climb to allow the fastest height gain.

The high initial rubber torque tends to roll the aircraft opposite to the direction the propeller turns, so a slight increase of incidence on one wing may be used for the first few seconds to counter this. The faster airspeed during this first phase also tends to make the model loop, because the lift from the wing increases with airspeed; the timer holds the tailplane with slightly more positive incidence during the 'power burst' to allow a steep climb without looping. It then re-trims the Wakefield to climb well under the reduced power.

Try this Now

Just like the engine of a car, a rubber motor is a heat engine; it stores energy and gets warm while being wound. To show this effect, take a thickish rubber band, quickly stretch it tight and hold it to your upper lip, still stretched. It feels warm, due to the energy you stored in it by stretching. Remove it, still stretched, and then release it to its normal length. Back on your lip it now feels cold, because it has released the stored energy (by pulling your hands together, actually, and slightly warming the air surrounding it).

Keep the Heat in

Having fully wound the rubber motor, some flyers now use an electrically-heated jacket wrapped round the fuselage to maintain the heat energy stored in it by winding. This is removed immediately before launch.

Other Classes

There is also an FAI class for smaller, rubber-powered aircraft, suited to smaller flying sites. Originating during the Second World War in France, and hence often known as Coupe d'Hiver, F1G models are allowed just 0.35 ounces (10 g) of rubber in an airframe weighing 2.4 ounces (70 g) or over. There is no limit on wing area.

Intended originally for younger flyers, the P-30 class grew in the

The tailplane in the tipped-up, dethermalised position. The spring-loaded aluminium triggers at the right control the various tailplane incidence angles during the climb and are operated by the timer. Tailplane mainspar is of tubular carbon fibre.

USA, but seems not to have attracted much interest outside. There is a 30-inch (760 mm) maximum wingspan and overall length, 0.35 ounces (10 g) of rubber are allowed in an airframe weighing 1.4 ounces (40 g) or over. The propeller must be an unmodified commercially-available plastic one of 9½ inches (241 mm) diameter or less, so this means it freewheels.

For those with flying sites of unlimited size, Open Rubber class aircraft have no limits on size or power. People like Phil Ball in Britain use models with 550 square inches (35 dm²) of wing area, weighing 6.3 ounces (180 g) and powered with 6.3 ounces of rubber turning a 30-inch (760 mm) propeller.

In 1977, 50 years after Lord Wakefield of Hythe presented model flying's premier trophy, Kim Dong Sik of North Korea won it at the World Championships at Roskilde in Denmark.

VERTICAL-CLIMBING, FLAT GLIDING

Perhaps the Rolls-Royces of free-flight competition, certainly in terms of cost, are FlC engine-assisted gliders. As with Formula 1 motor racing, power is all-important.

Most use glow-plug ignition engines, running at almost 30,000 rpm, and giving far more power for their size than the top racing-car engines. They may have an engine of up to 2.5 cm³, allowed to run for only seven seconds, and use a fuel of methanol and castor oil. Their special magic is that they start with a climb that would easily outpace the Space Shuttle, but then convert themselves to a silent, slowly-circling glider.

Uwe Glissmann of Germany demonstrates the perfect FlC vertical launch in the high temperatures at the World Championships in Yugoslavia in 1991.

Right Stafford Screen, Britain's most successful FIC flyer, launches a balsa-skinned aircraft in France in the mid-1980s. Notice the lower aspect ratio wing, built before high-tensile aluminium allowed narrower wings to be built.

Below Valery Strukov of the USSR in action at the 1989 World Free-Flight Championships at Cordoba, Argentina. It is vital to launch at exactly the right angle, both to the ground and to the wind.

Bottom 1989 World FIC Champion Randy Archer of the United States launches in the World Championships he won in Argentina. At the right is the sensitive electronic thermometer he uses to detect warming air and the arrival of a thermal.

Left Ken Faux's World Championship FIC engine-assisted glider climbs faster than the Space Shuttle for the 7-second burst of engine power allowed by the rules, but then becomes a slow-flying, thermal-riding glider. It is powered by an Italian AD. 15 25 cm³ glow-plug engine that turns a carbon-fibre bladed propeller at 30,000 rpm and produces more power for its size than the fastest Formular One racing-car engines.

51

About 8.3 seconds, the timer returns the tailplane to glide incidence position.

About 6.9 seconds, the timer pulls the tailplane down to a much more positive angle and the model pitches sharply nose-down into level flight. The timer moves the rudder to glide turn setting.

About 6.5 seconds, the timer cuts the engine (to ensure that the 7 seconds maximum engine run is not exceeded) and applies the propeller brake. The model is still climbing vertically.

Model is launched vertically, rudder straight, tailplane at slightly more incidence than glide setting.

THE SECRET OF SUCCESS

Persuading the engine to produce as much power as possible and to fly the aeroplane to the maximum height is the key to success in the FAI's class F1C. Fuel chemistry and engine running-time are restricted by the rules. Model weight depends on the total area and the engine size, but most are around 26¼ ounces (750 g) and have an area of about 590 square inches (38 dm²). Designing, developing, flying and competing with aircraft like this is a great challenge.

A pressurised fuel feed ensures that launch accelerations do not cause the engine to miss a beat. At today's engine speeds, the tips of the propellers are approaching supersonic speed and the centrifugal force on the blades is very high. Most propellers are moulded from carbon fibre and epoxy resin to withstand these loads. The blades usually fold after the engine stops, and the hubs are often titanium to take the forces involved.

Just as vital is the timeswitch. First it stops the engine, by 'dumping' the tank pressure, flooding the engine, and applying a propeller brake; then it trips the tailplane to pull the vertically-climbing aircraft through a quarter bunt into its slow glide; fractionally later, the timer resets the tail to the glide trim and resets the rudder to give a wide circle instead of a straight climb. Finally, at the end of the required 'max' flight time, it trips the tailplane to dethermalise the aircraft safely. Clockwork timers are common, but some sophisticated onboard computers have now appeared.

The original F1C models used tissue-covered wings, but as engine power and speeds increased, the wings tended to distort, or flutter, losing energy and creating consider-

Removing the glass-fibre cowling on Ken Faux's World Championships class F1C aircraft reveals the Italian AD .15 engine, mounted in a cast aluminium alloy 'pan' to reduce vibration. The engine exhaust is ducted rearwards under the wing and exits above it. The blades of the carbon-fibre propeller, moulded by Ken, are folded. A German-made Seelig clockwork time-switch operates the engine shut-off and propeller brake by releasing the wire cable seen under the wing leading edge. Other cables running to the rear operate the auto-rudder, the 'bunt' tailplane adjuster, and the dethermaliser.

able drag; or even breaking in flight. To counteract this effect, modellers changed to wings skinned with thin balsa sheet which increased their torsional stiffness; glass or Kevlar cloth further improved the situation. Today speeds are even higher and F1Cs use wings and tailplanes skinned with very stiff hard aluminium alloy (first used to cover full-sized helicopter blades by the MIL factory in the former USSR). This is glued under vacuum with epoxy resin to thin balsa sheet, the final composite material being used to cover a structure with carbon mainspar and balsa ribs.

Fuselages usually comprise a machined alloy front end, tying the engine, wing mount and tailboom together. The boom may be a tapered laminated tube of carbon cloth, Kevlar and hard aluminium alloy. Aeroplanes like this are not for the beginner, but to see one in action is inspiring.

A smaller FAI engine-powered class, F1J, exists. Maximum engine

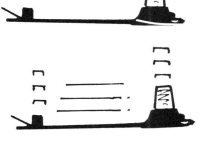

capacity here is 1 cm³, and minimum weight is 5.6 ounces (160 g). With the increasing popularity of CO_2 motors, class F1K was introduced in 1991 and has no limits, apart from a maximum gas tank capacity of 3 cm³. These motors are silent, allowing events to be flown close to housing areas.

Mighty Little Power

The first engine-powered free-flight models used two-stroke spark ignition motors, fuelled with a petrol and oil mixture. Around 1945, two-stroke diesels became popular and quickly took the place of spark motors. They needed no heavy batteries and ignition coil in the aircraft, and were thus much lighter.

Unlike car or truck diesels, model diesels did not have fuel injectors and complicated high-pressure pump; they used a fuel containing ether to ignite the paraffin providing the power. Ether ignites spontaneously when compressed by the upwards stroke of the piston, and strictly speaking the engines used in model aircraft are compression-ignition.

In the United States Ray Arden, a model engine manufacturer, introduced glow-plug ignition. Replacing the spark-plug, a glow-plug has a small platinum wire coil that is heated by an external battery. This ignites the fuel when the propeller is flicked and, once the engine is running, the battery can be removed. A combination of catalytic action between the alcohol-based fuel and the platinum, plus the residual heat of the red-hot coil, continues to ignite the fuel on every up-stroke. Today these engines are used for high-performance free-flight aircraft, though small diesels still power many scale and semi-scale models. Some of the original spark ignition engines, such as the classic Ohlsson .23, the Arden .19 and the Forster .29, still power lovingly

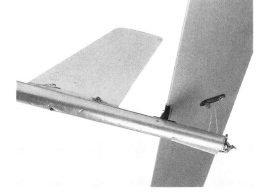

The tail surfaces of Ken Faux's F1C aircraft are covered with hard aluminium alloy bonded to thin balsa sheet, to reduce the risk of flutter during the high-speed climb. Instead of having a separate rudder, an all-moving fin is used to give less critical adjustments. The triggers at the rear of the fuselage operate the 'bunt' tailplane adjustment and the dethermaliser. The tailplane is in the D/T position.

At the end of the flight the timer operates the dethermaliser and the model descends safely.

duplicated vintage models flown at meetings of the Society of Antique Modelers.

The traditional means of starting a model engine is by flicking the propeller. With most F1C aircraft the folding blades make this impossible, so flyers use an electric or mechanical starter. The electric type consists of a car or motorbike starter motor, usually mounted in the flyer's tool-box, and with a hollow rubber fitting on the shaft to engage the propeller spinner. A foot-operated switch spins the starter motor, the nose of the aircraft is pushed into the rubber cup, turning the engine.

For contests, people tune the engines to give the maximum rpm, often using an electronic rev counter, or tachometer, to show the engine speed. These are either optically triggered by the propeller, or 'listen' to the exhaust note to measure the rpm.

Today's F1C aircraft have a problem. Even with seven seconds' engine run they climb so high – often over 600 feet (190 m) – that their long flat glide puts them outside many of the flying fields available.

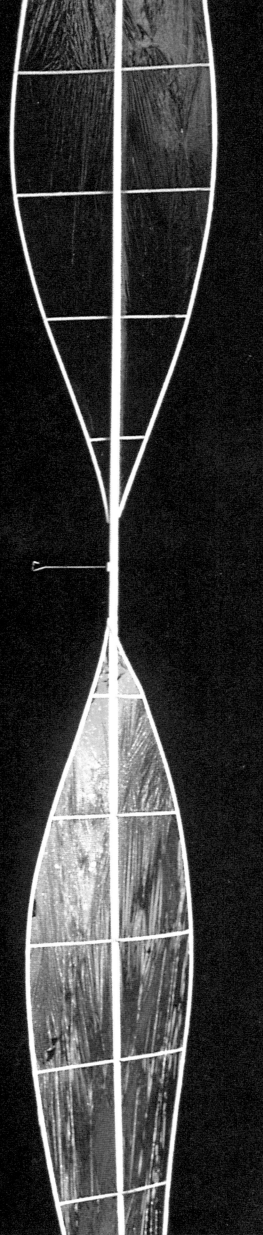

This 1993 F1D aircraft built by Robin Bailey uses no external wing bracing, but instead has leading and trailing edges of 0.035 inches (0.9 mm) balsa, tapering in depth from 0.1 inches (2.5 mm) at the wing root to 0.7 inches (1.7 mm) at the tips. Airframe weight is 1.15 grammes and the 18-inch (460 mm) loop of $\frac{1}{16} \times \frac{1}{24}$ inch (1.5 × 1 mm) FAI tan rubber weighs 1.4 grammes.

SLOW-MOTION WONDERS

Imagine huge transparent dragonflies, two feet across and shimmering like rainbows in the occasional shafts of sunlight that spear through the skylights of the vast cathedral-like space. The people holding them move like figures in a slow-motion film, for each fragile creation weighs just one gramme (28 of them to an ounce), and any fast movement would cause such air disturbance that they would be damaged.

Then one of the rubber-powered aircraft, for that is what we are looking at, flies free, very, very slowly, at about half a lazy walking speed. Its huge propeller turns at just 40 rpm, easily slow enough to count. It circles and climbs, but at first you think your mind has some kind of time delay; every-

This full-sized microfilm-covered propeller is from Robin Bailey's F1D aircraft. The diameter is 18 inches (460 mm), weight 0.2 grammes and it turns at about 40 rpm.

thing is still happening in slow-motion. The flight continues.

A quarter of an hour later the aircraft is near the dizzying cat-walk, 155 feet high among the girders of the Cardington airship shed, built in the 1920s to house the R100. Its flyer decides it is circling too near the sides of the metal-walled shed. Using a bright orange helium-filled balloon on a taut nylon fishing line, he very carefully brings the line close to nudge a wing of the slow-flying aircraft so it flies towards the centre again, and avoids hanging up on the sides of the building.

Twenty minutes later the ethereal-looking model begins to descend, its propeller still turning, and after 40 minutes of continuous powered flight the slowly-turning blade touches the floor and the aircraft subsides gently on to one wingtip like a tired butterfly.

The human-powered Gossamer Albatross cross-Channel aircraft flew on just a third of a horsepower, produced by its pilot Brian Allen. Designer Dr Paul MacCready and his team have a shared background in indoor model flying, and used the same techniques to achieve their breakthrough.

Robin Bailey and his FID microfilm model flying in the Cardington airship shed. Dr Robin Bailey works with British Aerospace Defence on the design and development of missile and weapon aerodynamics and structures; his expertise is in mathematical modelling. He has represented Great Britain on several outdoor and indoor free-flight teams at world championships.

Propeller hub and bearing of Robin Bailey's F1D aircraft. The thin black line along the side of the hollow motor stick is boron filament to provide extra stiffness. The thin post in front of the wing supports one of the twin nichrome wire braces above the fuselage.

Butch Hadland was one of Britain's greatest indoor flyers. Here he protects his F1D aircraft from damage in case the motor breaks while his assistant winds it. The major British trophy for indoor scale flying is named in his memory.

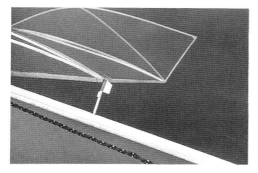

The wire rear motor-hook projects through the top of the fuselage to provide an anchor point round which the doubled bracing wire loops. A few thin strands of carbon fibre behind it reinforce the hollow tube to prevent it bursting when the rubber tension is held by the rear motor hook.

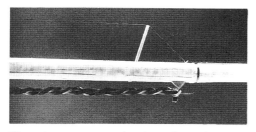

The small balsa block below the wing supports the twin wires that brace the motor stick. Moving and regluing it alters the tension in the wires, allowing the stick to bow more or less under maximum motor tension at launch. This alters the thrustline of the propeller and prevents the aircraft from stalling.

This view from above the tailplane (left) shows the balsa post glued to its rear edge that slides in a tube in the tailboom to alter its angle of incidence. The leading edge of the fin (right) has a similar adjuster.

THE MOST FROM THE LEAST

The gentlest of World Championships, class F1D, again has duration as its sole aim. The rules allow a wingspan up to 26 inches (650 mm) and a minimum airframe weight of 1 gramme without the rubber motor. The same technology was used for the man-powered Gossamer Albatross cross-Channel aircraft. For both projects it is vital to obtain the maximum flight efficiency from a limited amount of power, in one case a loop of rubber strip and in the other the muscles of a hard-pedalling athlete. Both aircraft are designed to be just sufficiently stiff to withstand the flying loads they will face, and their wings must give maximum possible lift for minimum drag, so that the available power is not wasted.

The microfilm used to cover these aircraft is about eight-millionths of an inch thick, far thinner than kitchen wrapping film, and is made by pouring a modified lacquer solution on to the surface of a tray of water. The solution spreads rapidly, like an oil film; it is then lifted very carefully on a wooden frame, and hung up to age and stabilise in a dust-free cupboard for a week or more.

The wing and tailplane structures are made from carefully selected balsa, chosen for lightness and stiffness, and often only about $\frac{1}{32}$ (0.8 mm) square. Building requires a steady hand, often a binocular magnifier, and good breath control. Weight-watching is crucial; therefore the glue is applied with a hypodermic needle. Some people add dye to it to spot any excess more easily. The finished structure is laid on to the microfilm, adhered with a little saliva, and a hot wire is used to melt the film outside the structure. Only one surface of the wing and tailplane is covered. Because the flying surfaces are still very flexible, many people brace them, like a girder bridge, by using nichrome wire less than half a human hair's diameter. Boron filament, a lightweight ultra-stiff material used in aerospace, may be carefully glued on to stiffen the fuselage and wings. Structural rigidity ensures the careful flight adjustments do not change and reduce duration.

The fuselage is a hollow tube of balsa, rolled from sheet wood about 0.013 inches (0.3 mm) thick, and the tapered tailboom is made from thinner wood. As the motor is beneath the tube, like the Delta Dart, more nichrome bracing above the fuselage withstands the tension of the fully-wound rubber.

F1D propellers are large, often two-thirds of the wingspan, and microfilm-covered. Their size tends to make the aircraft roll in the opposite direction to the propeller; the wing is usually built with more area on one side to cancel this effect.

The torque, or twisting force, that rubber produces is far greater when a motor is fully wound. However, the decline is not regular, but steep at first, before a steadier level of output is reached as the propeller unwinds, finally dropping steeply again at the end of the run. Harnessing this varying torque,

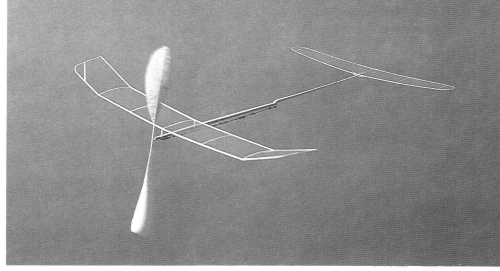

British indoor flyer Laurie Barr won the EZB (Easy Bee) duration event at the 1991 US Championships with a flight of over 23 minutes. His aircraft is covered with Polymicro Mylar film .00003 inches (0.0007 mm) thick, and weighs 1 gramme.

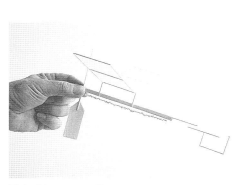

This Classroom Flyer is an ideal model to fly in small rooms. Built from a US kit produced by Gitlow it has a 9-inch (229 mm) wingspan.

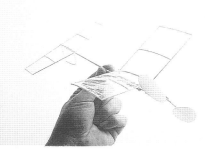

The Parlour Mite is one of a triple kit produced by Micro-X in the USA. Surprisingly long flights can be achieved in the average room at home, but keep the cat out.

Bruce Edwards launches a World Championships F1D aircraft. The wings are braced to the inverted V-shaped kingpost at their centre with nichrome wires .001 inches (0.02 mm) thick. The airspeed is about 2 mph (3.3 km/hr)

by matching the rubber motor cross-section with the propeller diameter and pitch, according to the ceiling height of the site, is the key to indoor flying. There is even a local climate indoors; a metal-walled building like the Cardington airship shed heats up on one side more than the other as the sun moves outside; this gives a slow circulation of air inside. and as a result, the aircraft may drift during a long flight, so they need to be steered by a carefully-plied balloon line. Using a highly-geared winder, and winding from the back, like the Delta Dart, motors often take 2,000 turns or so, and with a perfectly matched system the model would land as the rubber fully unwound.

More Indoor

Simpler classes also exist. EZB (Easy Bee) aircraft are often paper-covered; 18 inches (460 mm) is the maximum wingspan allowed, wing chord must be less than 3 inches (76 mm) and propellers must be of solid wood. Flights of 10 minutes are quite common in school halls or leisure centres, but beware of air conditioning. To a light model it can be like a hurricane.

MINIATURE FLYERS

In Britain maybe it was the boom in leisure centres that did it, springing up in the 1970s. Few of the wide range of so-called flying scale rubber kits that several manufacturers produced actually flew outdoors, but soon indoor model-flying meetings in these centres saw some scale models turning in flights of half a minute or more.

Bill Northrop, when editor of the US magazine *Model Builder*, regularly featured a centrefold full-sized plan for a flying scale model to the Peanut formula. This basically set a maximum wingspan of 13 inches (330 mm). Soon the hunt was on to find full-sized aircraft with a broad chord and short wingspan, so their model versions had as much wing area as possible, to give long durations. Even smaller Pistachio class models with an 8 inch (200 mm) wingspan presented a challenge.

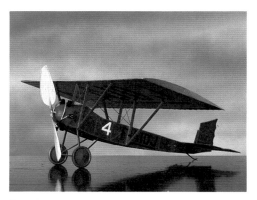

This Peanut scale model of the Farman Carte Postale was built by Ted Home. Its very low aspect ratio wing makes it ideal for the Peanut class, which limits wingspan to 13 inches (330 mm).

Models of several US home-built aircraft began to proliferate in Peanut contests. The Wittman Tailwind was one, but soon Lacey M-10s and the Fike, both slab-sided and squarish but with masses of wing area, started to win most events. In Britain Butch Hadland was the Lacey flyer *par excellence*, and his white aircraft with red pin-striping was the model to beat.

As with any aircraft, lightness is the secret of success. Propellers are much bigger than scale, to handle the rubber power more efficiently,

Aeronca K Peanut scale model by Nick Peppiat

Bellanca Skyrocket Peanut scale model by Peter Boys.

Unusual canard Rutan Vari-Viggen Peanut scale model by Nick Peppiat. The full-sized original was designed by Bert Rutan, a US model flyer whose later Voyager aircraft was the first to fly non-stop and unrefuelled round the world.

so hand-launching is the norm. With no pilot, tailplanes usually have to be enlarged from scale, too.

Some indoor sites have smooth ceilings with inset lights, so ceiling-scrubbing can be risked. With this technique models have rubber motors that give a climb higher than the available height, usually a sure way to hang up in the girders or lights at most venues. The slow, lightweight Peanuts just bounce off repeatedly before the torque drops and the descent starts.

Very small, lightweight, electric motors are a recent development. Fast-charge nickel-cadmium cells are used and most people use a tiny gearbox so the motor can swing a larger propeller at lower revs. In Britain, Derek Knight's KP-01 is the motor of choice.

Motors powered by carbon dioxide are another route. These have a

Thirteen-inch (330 mm) Peanut (left) and 8-inch (200 mm) Pistachio scale models of the Kalinin K-5 Soviet passenger aircraft of the 1930s by Div Masters.

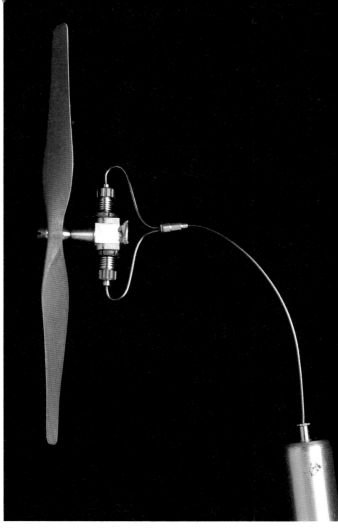

Shown here actual size is the miniature marvel G-6 twin cylinder CO_2 motor produced by Stephan Gasparin in the Czech Republic.

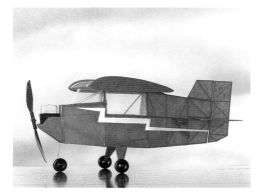

Peanut scale Stitts Baby Bird by Pete Smart. Full-sized original spanned a mere 6 feet 3 inches (1.9 m).

Nick Peppiat's North American P-51C Mustang Peanut model. The original was modified for post-war air racing from the fighter.

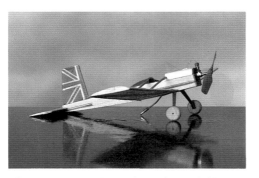

VP-1 Volksplane Pistachio scale model by Pete Smart uses a tiny Czech-built Gasparin G5 CO_2 motor.

Annemarie Hope-Cross holds father David's Peanut De Havilland Gipsy Moth as he winds at the New Zealand National Championships.

small on-board gas tank, filled from a fizzy drinks CO_2 capsule, and some of the motors produced in the former Czechoslovakia by computer-controlled machining are smaller than a fingernail.

While many of the structures are the traditional balsa strip and tissue type, foam polystyrene lends itself well to models of some of the more modern all-metal aircraft. A lightly sprayed finish helps to keep weight down and flight times high.

Scale free-flight also happens outdoors. In addition to rubber power, diesel, electric and CO_2 motors are used. As stability is marginal, with no pilot to keep control of an aircraft originally intended to have one, calm days are preferred. In the USA mass launches are popular; the last model to land is the winner. The reappearance of the Jetex type of motor means that again we can see the occasional jet fighter hissing across the sky in miniature.

OUTDOOR FREE-FLIGHT SCALE MODELS

Outdoor scale flying has a special appeal. In the United States the Inglewood Flitemasters introduced mass launch contests in the 1970s, with several dozen rubber-powered scale models taking to the air at once. Most outdoor scale models span 20 inches (500 mm) or more; many of them can takeoff from the runway like their original versions.

As well as the model's accuracy, its flight realism is also judged in competition; a model Bleriot flying at the scale speed of a Spitfire does not impress judges, so wing loadings must be kept light if a low airspeed is needed.

Czech flyers seem to have a special skill with outdoor scale rubber models. Lubomir Koutny in particular is renowned for immaculately-built models of military aircraft of the 1940s, with fuselages built from formers and multi-stringers, delicately airbrushed in camouflage colours to keep the weight down. His 1/20 scale plans include the Hawker Tempest V, Focke-Wulf Ta 152H and MIG-3, but also twins like the De Havilland Hornet and the Arado 240; Mike Woodhouse, whose address is in the suppliers' list on page 96, stocks these inspirations for the scale flyer.

In Britain, Charlie Newman's plan range includes such challenges as a twin-engined Handley-Page Hampden or Breguet 693, as well as simpler models like a Fiessler Storch or a Comper Swift. SAMS catalogue listing these and many others can be had from the address in the suppliers' list.

It is for scale models that the small, slow-running diesel engine is popular. Its exhaust does not dissolve the carefully applied finishes, so the heavy fuel-proofer needed for glow-plug engines is unnecessary. A diesel will turn a large propeller at low revs, too, so engines like the Mills .75, which first appeared over 40 years ago, are in demand again.

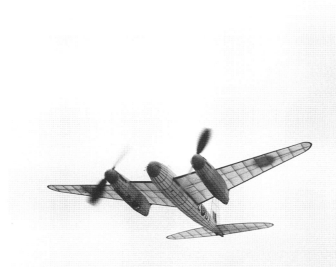

Above Bill Dennis adjusts the Mills diesel on his free-flight scale RE-8 reconnaissance biplane of 1916, at the 1991 British National Championships at RAF Fairford.

Left Mike Hetherington's rubber-powered Mosquito has more dihedral than the full-size original. This improves its stability, and counters the effects of air turbulence. The sun shining through the tissue covering emphasises the lightweight construction of this superb scale free-flight model.

Right A modified hand drill is used by Mike Hetherington to wind the twin rubber motors in each engine nacelle of his De Havilland Mosquito simultaneously. The model is held in a specially-built 'stooge', as Mike competes here at a contest in Italy.

Below The Jodel Bebe was a French homebuilt of the late 1950s. Don Knight built his from a Czech Igra kit and gets 40-second flights outdoors in calmish air. The model weighs 3 ounces (85 g), spans 24 inches (600 mm) and makes an ideal first rubber-powered outdoor scale aircraft.

Czech Junior World Championships team member Vladimir Kubes carries three Wakefields, tools, rubber and equipment in this compact case. Lightness and strength are important for boxes, for many are taken thousands of miles to championships all over the world.

BOXING CLEVER

Models deserve good boxes for storage and transport. They are delicate and any damage usually comes from careless handling, not flying. They don't take kindly to enthusiastic dusting, either, so keep them boxed while at home. Later, you will need strong but light boxes that can withstand car roof racks or airliner cargo holds.

A light-coloured box reflects the sun's heat and keeps the models and the rubber inside cooler than a dark one. People taking microfilm aircraft overseas pack them in a box with a clear Perspex side, so the contents can be seen without a customs man needing to open the box and disturbing the models inside.

For your first models a stout cardboard box will do the job. Cardboard from the packing boxes that fridges or TV sets are shipped in is ideal. Make a rough perspective sketch of the box you need, allowing a little more inside than the maximum component size of your model. Then draw the same box opened out flat, and add flaps on the ends and an overlapping lid. Mark this out on the cardboard and cut it with a Stanley-type knife and a metal straightedge.

Score on the inside the lines that will be folded, using a blunt screwdriver or a closed pair of scissors. Assemble your box with heavy staples, packing tape or brown gummed paper strip. Use small straps of Velcro to close the lid. You could give it a protective coat of polyurethane paint as a final touch.

Another handy box material is the foam-cored board used in graphics studios; they may give you offcuts or discarded boards. To make the

TOOLING UP

To build simple rubber models and hand-launched gliders you need a few basic tools. Most important is a *flat* building board. The Dart can be built on a piece of heavy cardboard, but plywood ¼ inch (6 mm) thick or thicker is needed for larger models. Graphics studios often discard material like Gatorfoam or Foamex – a card/foam plastic/card sandwich that is both light and stiff. Sundeala, a soft fibreboard used for partitions is another possibility. Whatever you use, make sure it is flat by laying a long ruler along it in various directions.

A stiff-backed razor blade, modelling knife or surgical scalpel are needed. Choose a blade with a fine point, but keep it sharp; a blunt edge is more likely to damage the wood or you than a sharp one. Hold the blade or scalpel near the cutting edge, like a pen, and steady the wood near the place you intend to cut it. *Never* cut towards your fingers, and always take several shallow cuts, rather than trying to cut through in one go. You may find that a razor plane is useful for carving and shaping wood.

Steel dressmaking pins, preferably with glass or plastic heads, complete your tool-kit. Keep them on a magnet.

Abrasive paper is needed for more advanced aircraft. Do not buy decorators' glasspaper, which is yellowish-gold and cracks easily. Choose either garnet paper (reddish-brown) or silicon carbide waterproof production paper. Grades 600, 320 and 120 will be useful. Stick your abrasive paper to one face of

a wooden block about 5 x 1½ inches (130 x 40 x 15 mm), and fold and stick it to the two long edges. Use rubber solution or double-sided Sellotape and press the paper to the wood by rolling it down hard with a bottle. Use this sanding tool to shape balsa.

Small pliers are needed for bending and cutting wire. Later, if there is wire to be joined, you will need a soldering-iron. Buy one with enough heat capacity for the job; a 60-watt iron will be fine for most piano wire. For cutting thicker wood a 6-inch (150 mm) Junior hacksaw is useful, or a razor saw, as are small files, drills and a 12-inch (300 mm) steel rule. A W-section safety rule will protect your fingers while cutting. You may need a longer steel straightedge later for stripping your own wood. If you want to treat yourself, buy a plastic self-healing cutting mat from a graphics supply store. A razor plane is handy for the larger shaping jobs on block balsa. For cutting plywood you may need a fretsaw; Abrafile-type flexible file-cum-saw blades are useful too, and can be used in the fingers. A small vice, perhaps with a vacuum-clamping base, acts as a second pair of hands. For doping tissue a 1-inch or ½-inch (25 or 15 mm) good quality brush is needed. Clean it in thinner after use, to keep it soft.

Improvised tools like clothes pegs, bulldog clips, masking tape and rubber bands can all hold jobs while the glue dries. Try to buy the best tools you can afford and they will last you all your modelling life.

folded edges with this you will need to cut a 45° groove halfway through it before folding.

Inside the box partitions can separate the model parts; at one end another wall can retain light tools and equipment so they cannot move and cause damage. When storing wings and tailplanes of models, rest them vertically on one edge, not lying flat, which induces warps. Otherwise make a flat frame from thick balsa and keep flying surfaces strapped to it with light rubber bands. These frames can slide into slots in the box to keep everything in place.

Store your boxed models well away from radiators or damp areas. Repair materials, dope, tissue, rubber, wire, stopwatch, retrieving compass, miniature binoculars, 12 volt soldering iron and a miniature drill

all come in handy on the flying field. A fold-flat carrying handle is useful, and a wide nylon shoulder strap leaves your hands free.

John Tipper carries three EZB indoor duration aircraft in this box, fitted with a Perspex front so the contents can be inspected by customs officers without opening. Slots cut in soft foam-rubber blocks hold the delicate parts in place.

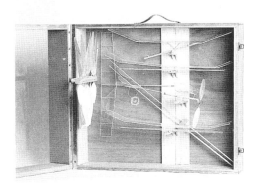

BUILDING THE DELTA DARTS

Now, for some practical experience, build and fly the Dart. The Dart is a proven flyer if built with care and accuracy. It is an excellent first model and has been adopted for educational programmes by model flying associations throughout the world. Well over three million have been successfully built and flown.

Flights of over one minute with a Dart are achieved. With the kits enclosed you should be able to make flights of over half a minute, and have fun competitions for the highest or longest flight.

Before building the Darts, check the kit contents; each will contain:

- building plan on lightweight paper
- propeller with hub bearing
- fuselage stick
- 10 lengths of balsa wood
- length of rubber motor

Keep the parts of each kit together, remember that balsa wood is fragile, and build one Dart at a time. Study the following pages carefully before beginning. Assemble the items you will need for building. They are listed opposite.

First build the fuselage and fin, together with the wing and tailplane. Tape the lightweight paper plan printed side down on to the building board, smoothing it as flat as possible. (You should be able to read the words **DELTA DART** the right way round.) The tape must not overlap any of the solid colour printed areas. If it is difficult to see the dotted lines when the plan is reversed, slip a sheet of white paper under the plan.

Study the plan carefully and you will see where dotted lines show the position of the framework. The lengths of balsa need to be cut to size, accurately, then glued on one side only, pressed down on to the plan and pinned in place to hold the part flat till the glue dries. Glue only the wood. Spread the glue with a finger (it's water soluble) or brush it on evenly before pinning down.

Now begin as follows:

1 Cut through the plan across the depth of the fuselage, on the line shown, at the point where the taper begins.

2 Take the fuselage stick (with the taper at one end) and position it correctly on the plan, with the taper on the bottom, on the opposite side to the position of the fin. Lift it off and apply glue only to the tapered area, on the side that will face the plan. Press it into the exact position on the plan, using two pins to hold it in place.

3 Cut the lengths of balsa to make the outlines of the fin, wings and tailplane, as shown in the main photograph. Note that the cuts must be at an angle to make accurate joints. To cut accurately, hold each piece against the plan, and mark the correct angle lightly with the knife. Lift the wood away and cut cleanly on another part of the building board, not the plan. Cut the longest pieces first so that you don't run out of wood. Keep the balsa strip and pieces of left-over lightweight paper for repairs.

TAILPLANE

FUSELAGE STICK

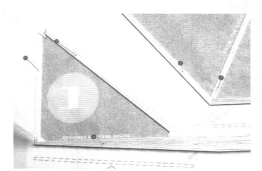

ITEMS YOU WILL NEED
- White PVA wood glue
- Adhesive tape, preferably masking tape, which is less tacky
- Pins, the round-headed type for building, and small pins for the rear motor hooks
- A *very sharp* modelling knife or scalpel. A blunt knife will not cut balsa wood accurately
- A *flat* board for building and cutting on. This needs to be larger than the paper plan and capable of taking pins. Thick cardboard, fibreboard, foam-filled cardboard or plywood are all satisfactory
- An inexpensive small brush for gluing
- Scissors

4 Starting with the fin, apply glue evenly to one flat side of each piece of balsa, and to the ends where they will touch another piece of wood. Press into position on the plan and pin into place. Continue, a piece at a time, and complete the tailplane and wing outlines. DO NOT yet glue the centre ends of the wing strips where they are circled on the main photograph. After gluing the outline strips in place, cut the three wing ribs to exact length. Cut one end to the correct angle first; then place this end in position against the outline and mark the opposite end with the knife blade to get both the length and angle right.

WING

FIN

5 There are five triangular flaps of paper at the acute angles on the fin, tailplane and wingtips. These need to be cut where indicated and glue applied to the paper triangles, which are then folded back on to the wood, pressing down firmly. This reinforces the joints.

6 Check everything is completed, allow the glue to dry, then cut carefully around the outside edges of the fin, tailplane and wing. Remove them from the board. Before removing the rest of the plan note the dotted lines indicating where to fix the tailplane and wing on the fuselage.

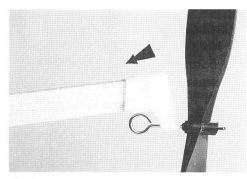

1 Push the propeller-bearing socket on to the fuselage stick. It should be a firm fit. If it is too tight, gently trim the balsa until you can push it right on.

2 Measure 1¼ inches (32 mm) from the front of the propeller-bearing socket and mark on top of the fuselage stick the position for the leading edge of the wing (see main picture). Glue under the centre balsa strip in the wing, and place it on top of the fuselage stick. Press it into position and pin to the fuselage.

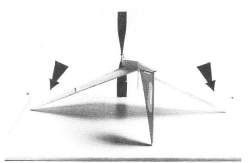

3 Turn the Dart over and press the wings down firmly. Position over the building board and with the propeller and fin vertical, and just touching the board, pin the wingtips to the board. This determines the correct dihedral angle. When you are pinning the wingtips down, you may need help to keep the fin and propeller vertical, or use some small weights or blocks.

ASSEMBLING THE DART

To complete the building of the Dart, the next stage is to assemble the wing and tailplane with the fuselage and fin. At the same time the correct dihedral angle for the wing is established. Study the main picture and follow the sequence above.

4 Apply glue generously to the wing roots where indicated by the arrows.

5 Apply glue to the single dotted line down the centre face of the tailplane. Turn it upside down and press and pin it into position on the tapered rear end of the fuselage stick. Ensure that it is square with the fuselage and parallel with the building board.

6 It is important to allow the glue to dry for at least an hour and preferably overnight.

7 When the glue is thoroughly dry, remove the pins and inspect the assembled model. Check that the wing and tailplane are fixed firmly. If not, you must repeat the previous procedure and apply some extra glue.

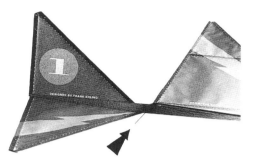

8 If all is satisfactory, carefully push a small pin into the fuselage stick at an angle of about 45°. It should be positioned at the leading edge of the tailplane, and forms the rear motor hook.

9 Take the length of rubber strip, and tie the ends with an overhand knot. Pull tight. To make sure the knot does not come undone, tie another knot with the loose ends. If you wish the rubber can now be lubricated (see page 31).

10 Now suspend the rubber from the front and rear hooks and you are ready for trimming flights.

FLYING THE DART

When one or both of the Darts are complete and checked, try some test flights. For flying outdoors, choose a calm day and avoid damp air or moist ground, as this will shrink the paper covering and distort your Dart. The Dart is a light model and will be affected by anything stronger than a light breeze. Fly in a clear, open space; parkland or a large field are ideal. Large sports halls are good for indoor flying.

Carry the Dart with care, preferably in a box; like most model aircraft it is light and therefore fragile. For test flying, known by model flyers as 'trimming', take with you masking tape and scissors and a small amount of modelling clay. The Dart is designed to be inherently stable in flight but some adjustment may be needed.

Follow the instructions and watch each flight carefully. Only make trim adjustments one at a time, and repeat flights to check that the flying pattern is consistent.

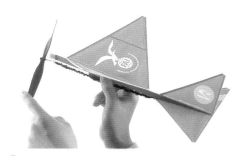

2 To fly, hold the fuselage stick in one hand and one tip of the propeller with the other. Keep the wingtips of the model parallel with the ground and its nose slightly up.

1 Hold the model by the fuselage under the wing and wind the motor by turning the propeller clockwise when seen from the front. Pull back on the rubber as you apply the first few turns to avoid bunching round the front hook. Start with 50 turns.

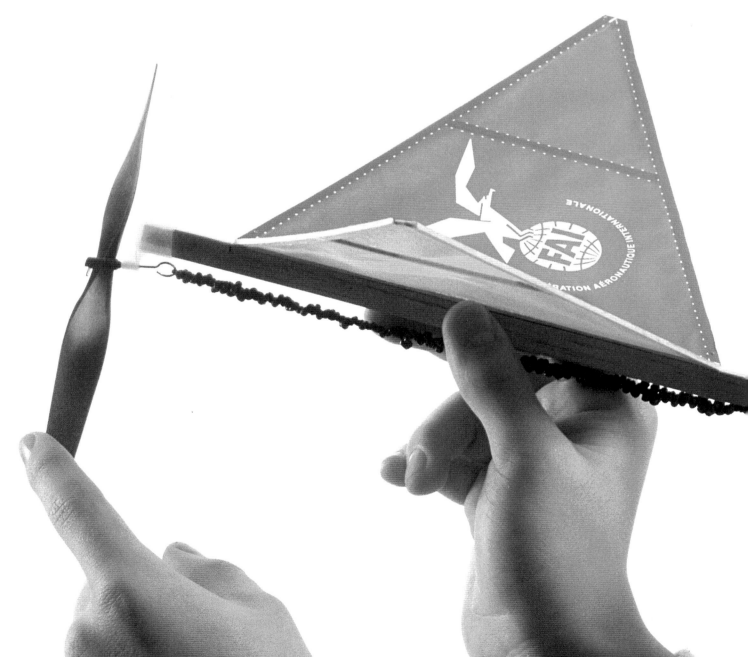

TRIMMING

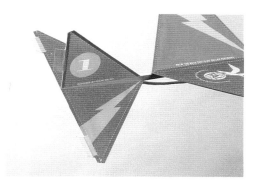

3 If outdoors, face the model into the wind, after checking its exact direction with a handkerchief or a few blades of grass thrown into the air. Release the propeller fractionally before launching the model with a gentle push. Make sure you launch smoothly.

Stalling under Power
If when you launch your Dart it flies in a series of up and down movements, as on a switchback, it is 'stalling'. Carefully twist the thin part of the propeller bearing assembly further to the right, and try another flight.

Lack of Climb
If your Dart fails to climb, you will need to add 'elevator' trim tabs. Make these from ¾-inch (20 mm) wide masking tape cut into 2-inch (50 mm) lengths. Attach two tabs to the trailing edge of the tailplane; stick one long edge of the tape to the bottom of the wood and then fold the tape to double back and stick to itself. Turn these tabs up slightly (you may have to bend them more than you want at first, as the tape is slightly springy), and try another flight. Increase the angle of the tabs as needed to make your Dart climb.

4 The Dart should climb gently and start to turn. If the flight looks good increase the number of turns on the propeller to 100. The model should climb higher and turn. Watch what happens when the power runs out and the Dart begins to glide; this should be smooth.

5 If your flights are satisfactory, increase the number of turns each time until you feel the rubber motor is tight. Do not be tempted to over-wind and break the motor. Check each time before you launch that the rubber motor is not bunching into knots against the fuselage stick, and that the propeller is free to turn.

Stalling when Gliding
If your model flies smoothly under power, but up and down when gliding, add small amounts of modelling clay to the nose until you achieve a smooth glide.

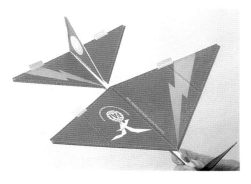

Diving Turns
If your aircraft dives as it turns, add 'aileron' trim tabs to the wings to correct this. Turn the tab slightly downwards on the wing you want to raise, on the inside of the turn, and upwards on the opposite wing.

Controlling the Turn in Flight
If you want to adjust the tightness of the turn in flight, add a rudder trim tab on the fin. To increase the turn to the right, turn the rudder trim tab to the right; at the same time move the right wing aileron tab slightly down and the left one slightly up. Reverse this procedure for a left turn.

Make all adjustments gradually, and watch the flight of your Dart carefully to see the effect of the changes. When the turn is correct, check regularly between flights that all trim tabs are in the correct position.

GETTING MORE FROM THE DART

Once you have trimmed your Dart, you will want better flights. The key factor is the rubber motor; more turns mean more power and higher and longer flights. Lubricating the motor helps, but 'stretch winding' produces the best results, and a geared winder piles on the turns quickly.

'Fine tuning', balancing the propeller, oiling the propeller bearing and experimenting with different rubber motors all help the expert to achieve flights over the 'magic minute'. 'Getting more' also means looking after your model and enjoying the fun of simple competitions.

NAME	1	2	3	4	5	6	7	TOTAL (Seconds)
PLACE *Barkston Heath* DATE *25th May*								
Andrew	17·1	20·2	4·4	12·0	29·1	7·0	15·3	93·7
Sam	4·2	15·5	19·0	31·1	12·0	21·1	14·5	101·2
Sally	22·2	9·3	7·7	18·6	25·6	16·9	14·0	97·3.

COMPETITIVE FUN

Instead of simply flying their model aircraft, many people find that it adds a lot of enjoyment to time the flights. Trying to squeeze a second or two of extra time in the air from an aircraft you made yourself helps you to find how small adjustments can make a visible difference to the flight.

Competing against yourself and the stopwatch like this is fun. When several of you do this together you have a competition. This can simply be a series of flights which you time and note down. Take turns to time each other. Discarding the two lowest times of, say, seven flights lets you make the odd mistake without ruining your score. Add the total of the five best.

Rubber Motors

The motor with your kit is 22 inches (560 mm) of ⅛ inch (3 mm) flat rubber strip, which makes up into a 10- inch (255 mm) loop. It is best lubricated (see page 31); it should take about 250 turns winding by hand and over 400 if stretch wound. When using new rubber, increase the turns gradually with each flight. Always keep it clean, wash with soap if it gets gritty, and store it in a cool, dark place.

It will break eventually, and it is best to buy extra lengths of rubber from a model shop or one of the suppliers listed at the end of the book. Experiment with longer loops of rubber, say 12,14 and 16 inches (300, 350 and 400 mm), to get more turns, but they must be stretch wound. Different widths of rubber are obtainable; 0.1 inch (2.5 mm) wide will allow more turns and longer flights, but with less height, useful indoors in halls.

Stretch Winding

The single most important route to better performance is stretching the rubber in order to wind on more turns. You will need a winder and a helper. Unhook the motor from the rear of the Dart, hook on to the winder and stretch the rubber as far as you comfortably can, say five times its unstretched length, while your helper holds the Dart securely. Wind on the turns, counting the number as you apply them (remember the winder is geared). Move towards the aeroplane as you wind on the last half of the turns you decided on, till you arrive back at the rear hook as you finish. Grip the rubber tightly near the winder hook, release a few turns to free the end of the loop and unhook the winder. Hook the rubber back on the rear hook.

Fine Tuning

Check the balance of the propeller; if it is out of balance it will cause vibration and waste power. Balance it horizontally on the shaft; if one blade seems heavier, add a small piece of masking tape to the tip of the other blade, till the propeller balances.

The free running of the propeller will be helped by adding a drop of light machine oil to the bearing, but avoid getting any oil on the rubber. Sandpapering the underneath edges of the fuselage stick smooth and round saves scuffing the rubber motor.

Care and Maintenance

Keep your Darts protected in a box. Find or make one from cardboard. A size of 14 × 12 × 6 inches (350 × 300 × 150 mm) will contain both Darts, with the one on top upside down and facing the opposite way.

Don't let the Dart get damp or wet, as the lightweight paper will shrink and warp the structure.

Ensure the structure of the Dart remains firm. Reinforce the wing, tailplane and fin joints with glue when necessary. Breaks in the balsa structure can be repaired by gluing on short splints made from spare strips of balsa. Mend tears in the paper by patching the unprinted side with thin paper using PVA white glue.

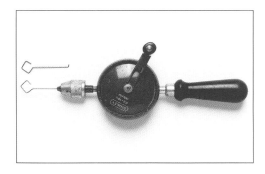

Winders

Inexpensive geared winders are obtainable from mail-order model suppliers. Most have a ratio of 6:1; higher ratios are available. A good alternative is a standard hand-drill. Bend a length of steel wire into a hook. For safety, make sure a small right angle is bent at the other end of the hook, so it cannot pull out of the drill chuck. Check the gear ratio (usually 3.5:1) in order to calculate the number of turns being applied.

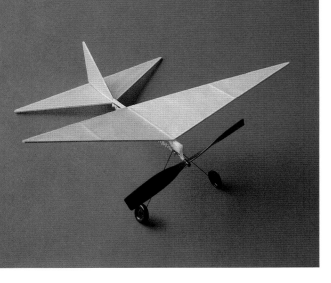

AFTER THE DART

With the experience of building and flying the Darts under your belt you're ready to hit the free-flight contest trail or build that scale Spitfire. Well, not quite. Something like one of the models on the next few pages is a better move. You will find that making a good job of build-

The Gyminie Cricket is the British Model Flying Association's follow-on model after the Dart. Designed by Mike Colling to be flown in a school gymnasium or a large hall, it uses the same moulded nylon propeller as the Dart, but has a lighter and more delicate balsa strip structure, built first on a plan and then covered with lightweight tissue paper. Kits can be purchased from the BMFA, Chacksfield House, 31 St Andrews Road, Leicester LE2 8RE.

The Peck Rise-Off-Ground model is kitted in the United States and uses thin card ailerons, elevator and rudder to adjust the flight. It is suitable for indoor flying after you have some experience building and flying the Delta Dart. An annual Peck ROG contest is run in Britain by SAMS, from whom kits can be obtained.

Left A finished Dart R.O.G. model

ing it and getting better and better flights from it will be quite hard at first, but the enjoyment you will have doing so is unique.

One way to go is via a hand-launched glider like those on pages 72 and 85. Some are intended for indoor flying in a school hall or a leisure centre. Outdoors a site a bit bigger than a football field can contain most flights, until you start to look for thermals to launch into.

Alternatively a good next step is to build one of the indoor rubber models on this page. Either buy a kit or build the Dart ROG model from the plan opposite. Another route is to build an outdoor rubber-powered model from a kit. Look in model shops or mail order catalogues and choose a simple model with a wingspan of 24–30 inches (600–750 mm).

Dart ROG

The same building techniques for the Delta Dart can be followed for this delightful rise-off-ground model. Designed by Robin James as a lighter development of the Delta Dart, it can be flown in sports halls or out-doors on a still, dry day. It is built onto tissue paper over the plan and uses the same propeller as the Dart.

Tools and Materials

As well as the tools used for building the Delta Dart, you need a small pair of pliers and wire cutters. Use PVA glue or aliphatic resin adhesive. The following materials are required: Sheet of lightweight tissue paper. (Almost any type will do, but you need to see the plan through it).

A strip of ¼ × ⅛ inch (6 × 3 mm) medium balsa and two 36-inch (900 mm) lengths of ¹⁄₁₆ × ¹⁄₁₆ inch (1.5 × 1.5 mm) hard balsa strip.

A length of 22 s.w.g. steel wire for the undercarriage, and a scrap of thin plastic sheet for the wheels. If you wish, you can buy ready-made plastic wheels and an extra pro-peller (MPC 6 inch) from mail order supplier SAMS.

A length of ³⁄₃₂ inch (2 mm) rubber strip for the motor.

CONSTRUCTION SEQUENCE

1 Photostat or trace the plan on the page opposite. Tape or pin it to the building board.

2 Cut the fuselage stick from ¼ × ⅛ inch (6 × 3 mm) balsa. Note the angle must be cut at the rear to form the angle of incidence for the tailplane. Cut and glue the extra nose piece in place.

3 Cut accurately the lengths of ¹⁄₁₆ (1.5 mm) square balsa for the wing, tailplane and fin framework. Keep the parts together to ease assembly.

4 Stretch and tape the sheet of tissue over the plan.

5 Follow the same sequence of assembly as for the Delta Dart.

6 Allow to dry thoroughly and cut the tissue around the outlines of the frames and remove from the board. Note, as on the Delta Dart, the small triangular rein-forcing gussets at the wing, tailplane and fin tips must be cut, folded over and glued.

7 Assemble as for the Delta Dart. Reinforce the fuselage to wing joints well with glue. Fix the tailplane into position, checking it is square with the fin, and leave for the glue to set.

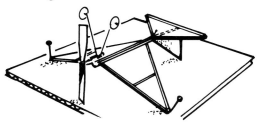

8 Bend and cut the wire for the under-carriage following the pattern on the plan. Form the right angle bend at the top last. Fit on the wheels. To retain them bend the wire up neatly, or else push on short lengths of plastic insulation from fine electrical wire. To make your own wheels, cut them from thin plastic sheet. Discarded packaging is a good source of material. Use a suitable sized coin to cut round. Make the centre hole with a pin.

9 Remove the model from the board and then remove the propeller and its bearing. The top of the undercarriage slides into slots in the socket, which is then pushed back onto the fuselage. Finally push a pin in position under the rear fuselage to form the motor hook. Make up a loop of ³⁄₃₂ inch rubber for the motor and fit it between the hooks.

10 Test fly your model as you did the Delta Dart, Once you have successfully trimmed it with hand launches, try flying off the ground. You may need to turn the tailplane trim tabs up, or increase them in size.

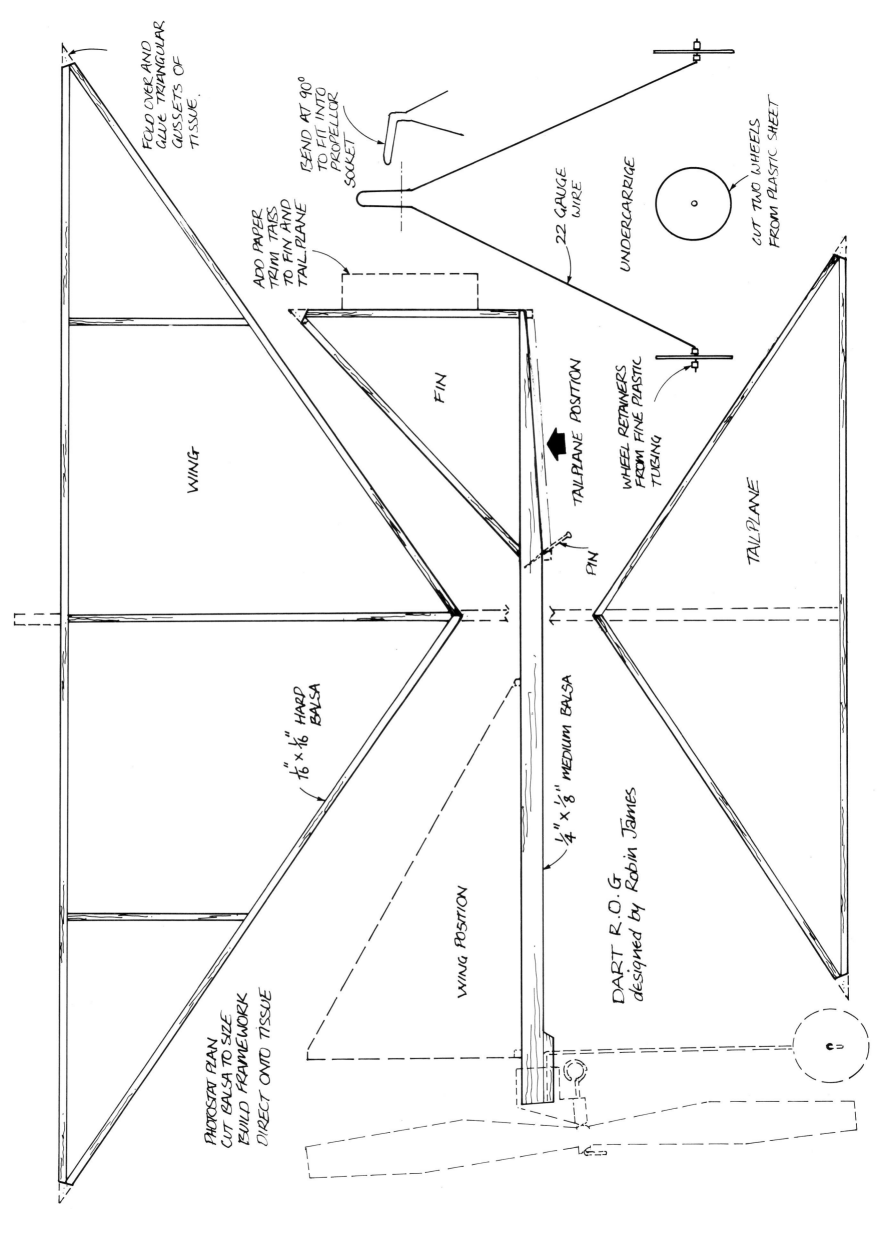

FOLD OVER AND GLUE TRIANGULAR GUSSETS OF TISSUE.

BEND AT 90° TO FIT INTO PROPELLOR SOCKET

ADD PAPER TRIM TABS TO FIN AND TAILPLANE

22 GAUGE WIRE

UNDERCARRIGE

CUT TWO WHEELS FROM PLASTIC SHEET

WHEEL RETAINERS FROM FINE PLASTIC TUBING

WING

FIN

TAILPLANE POSITION

PIN

TAILPLANE

$\frac{1}{16}$" × $\frac{1}{16}$" HARD BALSA

$\frac{1}{4}$" × $\frac{1}{8}$" MEDIUM BALSA

WING POSITION

PHOTOSTAT PLAN
CUT BALSA TO SIZE
BUILD FRAMEWORK
DIRECT ONTO TISSUE

DART R.O.G.
designed by Robin James

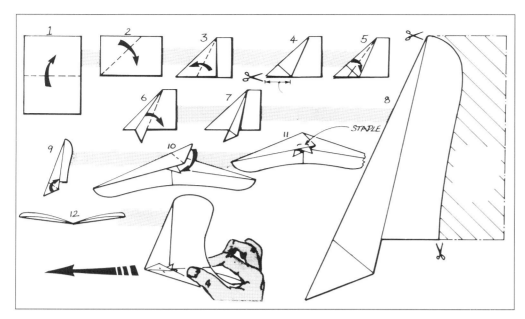

Fig. 6. Fold again to look like Fig. 7 and repeat both steps for the other side.

6 Holding wingtips and leading edges together, cut wing shape to outline shown, by eye or by tracing. Fold one flap up as in Fig. 9, leave other flap flat.

7 Open the wings to lie flat, as in Fig. 10.

8 Fold the small projecting flap A back and under flap B. It will now look like Fig. 11, which shows the underside of the glider. Make sure all folds are well flattened, then put a single staple through the centre of all the layers of paper.

9 Bend the staple slightly to give a small dihedral angle to the wings, as in Fig. 12. Use a fingernail to smooth a slight billow into each wing.

10 Hold your Paperang by the centre section and launch firmly and slightly nose down. If it turns, increase the camber of the wing on the inside of the turn until you produce a straight glide.

Start with a sheet of A4 typing paper.
1 Fold it in half lengthways.
2 Fold down front and rear corners away from each other.

3 Fold flaps forward along the midlines.
4 Make a single cut along the centre line.
5 Fold flap again along its midline as shown in Fig. 5. It should now look like

ARM POWER

The simplest sort of model is a hand-launched glider. Paper gliders fly well. Dr Edmund Hui, a computer consultant and hang-glider pilot, who learnt origami at school in Hong Kong, combined his skills to design the Paperang. Try it; its 30 foot (9.7 m) flights easily beat the school-boy paper dart.

The magazine *Scientific American* has organised international events for paper aeroplanes, and the FAI has a specification for simple paper glider contests. Models can be cut or folded from a single A4 (297 × 210 mm) sheet of paper of 80 grams/M^2 density or less. Glue and ballast is allowed, and models must be hand-launched from a maximum height of 6½ feet (2 m). The longest single flight time wins, and there are under-16 and over-16 classes.

Slightly more advanced is the wood and paper glider; one is the AeroGlide, used in the British Model Flying Association's education programme. Mike Colling, who runs the programme, designed the Flinger, or rather three of them, from a single sheet of 1/16 inch (1.5 mm) balsa, 3 × 36 inch (76 × 914 mm), plus a length of 1/8 × 3/8 inch (3 × 9 mm) balsa. Cut as shown, and add some glue and modelling clay for nose weight.

There are several kits for 'chuck gliders'. They are a good way to learn the rudiments of trimming. DPR Models' Chuckie is one. DPR's director Dave Rawlins runs Chuckie competitions for under-16s all over Britain, and a model like this is a good way to start on a lifetime's model flying. More refined hand-launched gliders have flown an incredible minute and a half in a huge airship shed. Lee Hines of California set this record in the

The DPR Models Chuckie is a simple all-balsa hand-launched glider built from a kit. All parts are pre-cut, and everything, including balsa cement, ballast and even sandpaper is included.

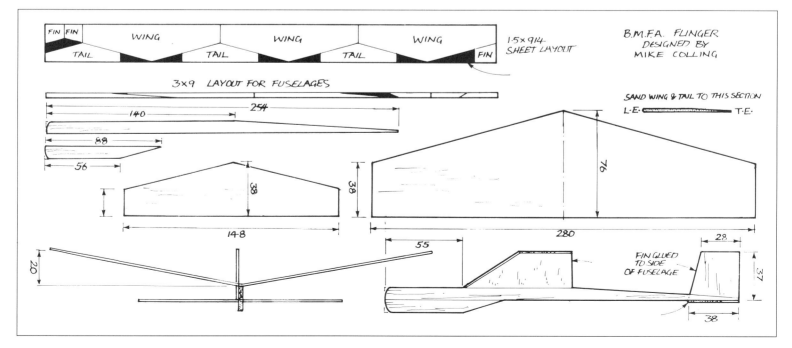

1970s with his classic Sweepette design.

Today's competition indoor HLG is a deceptively simple-looking aircraft. Made from low-density balsa, the wing is carved and sanded to an undercambered airfoil section to give a very slow glide. However, a high duration will result only from a launch to the ceiling of the hall, and an undercambered wing will cause a loop if thrown hard. A thin and light wood wing will flutter at high speed, too. An insoluble problem? Not with carbon fibre. This light material greatly stiffens the fuselage and wing. Cutting the rear half of the wing at its centre allows the high launch speed to blow the wing into a flatter airfoil, killing the looping tendency. It then droops to its normal section as the airspeed slows.

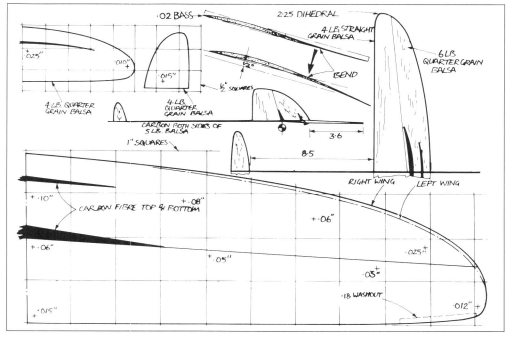

Mark Drela set a US national indoor hand-launched glider record of 93.7 seconds in 1980 with his 20-inch (500 mm) Upstart 4. Carbon fibre stiffens the balsa fuselage, tailplane and wing, but keeps the total weight to only 5.5 grammes. The front half of the wing is carved from stiff light quarter-grain balsa, with the flexible rear half from straight-grain wood.

GETTING THE BEST FROM HAND-LAUNCHED GLIDERS

The glider cannot be too large or too heavy, so they are usually between 12 inches (300 mm) and 24 inches (600 mm) wing span, weighing between ½ ounce (14 g) and 2 ounces (60 g). Wings, tailplane and fin are usually carved and sanded from soft, light sheet balsa; fuselages are from harder balsa for strength, spruce or a tapered fibreglass tube, originally the thin tip of a fishing rod.

Strong and accurate glue joints are vital; the throw puts a tremendous strain on them, so use a five-minute epoxy like Araldite Rapid or Devcon on the wing/fuselage and dihedral joints.

Flying
Before we start, think what we are trying to achieve. Grip the model firmly, run a few paces as if throwing a ball and then heave it for all you're worth. Ideally it shoots up vertically, loses momentum and then transitions into a gentle floating glide. Fine, but how to make it happen?

First check the model critically. Make sure the wings and tail are warp-free, and everything lines up properly. Models glide better in circles rather than a straight line, and stay in sight longer. For a right-hander a left-gliding model gives a safer trim (less likely to crash), so if you are left-handed reverse all the following help. The throw gives a right bias on the climb before the model swings into a left glide. To help that

left glide glue on the tailplane so the left tip, looking from the rear, is about ⅛ inch (3 mm) higher than the right. Bend the rear ¼ inch (6 mm) of the fin slightly to the left to form a rudder.

Ensure the balance point is correct. Fifty per cent of the root chord is normal. To get this right, mark this point and balance the model with your fingers under the wings. Add modelling clay to the nose till the model balances level.

Choose a calm day and a soft grassy field to absorb any hard landings. At first try a few gentle and level launches into wind to establish a basic glide trim. The launch should be like a slowly-thrown dart; the model glides smoothly away, with a slight curve to the left, to land about 10 metres from you. If it stalls or dives, try again before altering anything; your launch may have been too nose up, too fast, too slow or angled too hard at the ground. Add a little more noseweight to cure a stall, or bend up the rear ¼ inch (6 mm) of the tailplane to cure a dive.

Now for a hard throw. Warm up your arm first by throwing a tennis ball a few times. Grip the fuselage with your thumb and second finger, and put your index finger against the rear edge of the right-hand wing; most hand-launched gliders are reinforced here. Take a few steps, draw back your arm and throw hard into the wind. If you are lucky the glider will follow the flight pattern described earlier. One of the following is more likely.
a) The model shoots straight up, stalls and dives into the ground. The adjustment may be fine, but perhaps you are not throwing hard enough. Try again, but

bias it slightly to the right to make it climb at a shallower angle.
b) The throw banks the model sharply right. Are you aiming directly into the wind? Add a little more left rudder and try again.
c) The throw is fine but the glider develops a stall later in the flight. Add a little more noseweight or a bit more left rudder if the glide is too open.
d) The throw is fine but the glide tightens, finally spiralling into the ground. Try less rudder, remove a little noseweight or gently bend up the rear edge of the tailplane a little. Another adjustment used *in moderation* for this fault is to warp down the rear edge of the left wingtip. This is called 'wash-in'. All these adjustments should be made in very small amounts, maybe ⅟₁₆ inch (1.5 mm) at a time, as we are flying small models.
e) On a hard throw, the model loops straight over. If the first glide tests are good, this is unlikely. The remedy is to move the balance point (centre of gravity) back by removing some noseweight, and to bend the rear edge of the tailplane down to restore the glide.
f) The model dives straight in. Bend up the rear edge of the tailplane to make it climb; if it then stalls on the glide, add some more noseweight.
To add to the fun, do a series of flights on a calm evening, and time them with a stopwatch to see how effective your adjustments are. Thirty seconds with a 'chuck glider', is quite reasonable, 40 is wonderful and over 50 puts you in the experts' class.

ENDURING FAVOURITES

When Louis Heath designed the Achilles and larger Ajax rubber models for Eddie Keil's London company KeilKraft to kit at the beginning of the Second World War, he probably did not imagine that they would still be in production over 50 years later. They first appeared in mid-1940, just after the Battle of the River Plate, when two British cruisers, HMS *Ajax* and HMS *Achilles*, cornered the German pocket battleship *Graf Spee* off Montevideo in Uruguay; her captain later scuttled her. Patriotism was running high in Britain. At a low ebb in the war any victory was a big morale booster, so KeilKraft named its new models after the victorious warships. Built lightly and accurately, they were many a schoolboy's introduction to a model flying career that would last a lifetime.

In the 1950s Albert Hatfull modified the kits for KeilKraft. Today Amerang, who now own the company, still produce the Ajax and Achilles, though the price of the latter has gone from 3s 8d (18 pence in today's money) to £6.95. There are other changes in the kits, too. A heavier but simpler to manufacture plastic propeller replaces the light balsa blank that was produced on a spindle carving machine for the first kits; heavier solid plastic wheels are in today's kits, instead of the original hollow ones made from two moulded celluloid shells. Tubes of balsa cement and tissue paste were included in early kits, too.

Nostalgic enthusiasts still return to their roots and build these enduring favourites, usually discarding the plastic injection-moulded parts that owe more to manufacturing convenience than airworthiness. Many of them introduce their children to the same thrill of actually making something that flies in the face of video-centred pre-packaged entertainment.

While not truly beginners' models, kits like the Ajax and Achilles are a good second step towards building more complex free-flight models.

This 1941 *Aeromodeller* magazine advertisement for the KeilKraft Ajax underlines the model's flying qualities. In it builder Michael Jennings writes: 'I entered an Ajax in the Gamage Cup and gained second place. Flight was timed out of sight directly above takeoff for 17 minutes 48 seconds. It was the very sound design of your model which decided me to build and enter it. My only regret is that I have not heard anything of it since it flew away into the clouds.'

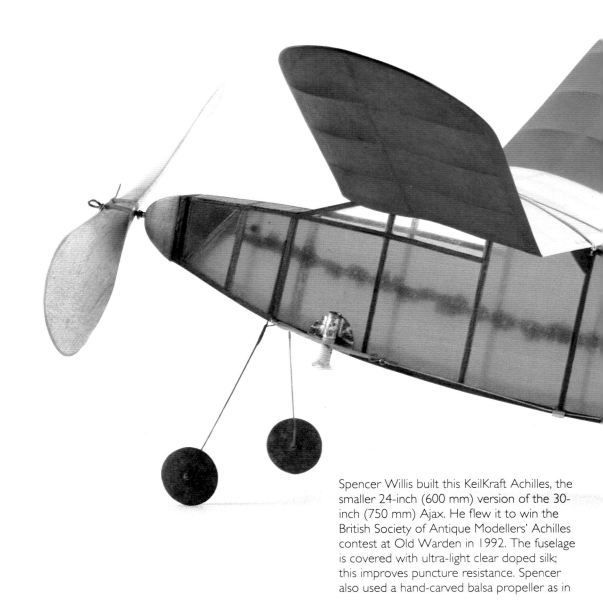

Spencer Willis built this KeilKraft Achilles, the smaller 24-inch (600 mm) version of the 30-inch (750 mm) Ajax. He flew it to win the British Society of Antique Modellers' Achilles contest at Old Warden in 1992. The fuselage is covered with ultra-light clear doped silk; this improves puncture resistance. Spencer also used a hand-carved balsa propeller as in

BUILDING FROM A KIT

Building a more complex model than the Dart requires rather different techniques, and we will look at the KeilKraft Ajax kit to illustrate some of them.

Three points are the key to building a successful flying model: accuracy, strength and lightness.

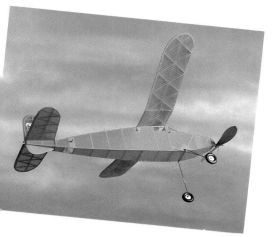

Derek Havendon built this modified version of the KeilKraft Ajax. He used geodetic wing ribs to provide extra warp resistance, a carved balsa propeller and lightweight moulded celluloid balloon type wheels instead of the solid plastic ones supplied in the kit today.

Accuracy

Before you cut any wood look at the plan and read the instructions till you understand the various points you will meet. Check the kit contents, wood sizes and printed or die-cut sheet parts and make sure you know where they all go. Try to understand what they are where they are, and what job they do.

Good close joints, accurate but not forced, with just a thin film of adhesive between the faces, are the secret of a warp-free aircraft. If a piece of wood needs to be bent, steam it to shape rather than forcing it round and expecting the glue to hold it. Sooner or later the natural springiness of the wood will cause problems. Similarly, if a piece of strip wood is warped in the box, it is better to steam it straight instead of gluing it that way.

Strength

Balsa wood can vary in density and grain along its length and width. The stiffness across the grain of a sheet depends on how it was cut from the log.

Quarter-grain wood looks speckled, is stiff across the width of a sheet, and used for flat parts like ribs and flat-plate fins and tailplanes. Straight-grained wood shows lengthways lines and is more flexible across the width; it is used cut into narrow strips for such parts as spars and longerons. There is more about this on page 28.

As quality control in many kits is poor, the wood may not be the best for the job. Select the hardest, stiffest strips for the fuselage longerons and wing spars. Try to keep the lightest ends of the strips at the tail of the fuselage and the wingtips. An experienced free-flight modeller will be able to advise you whether or not to buy replacement wood.

Lightness

Lighter aircraft fly better if they have enough strength. Keep the extremities – tail surfaces and wingtips – light. The structure is subject to less load there, so less strength is needed.

the first Achilles kits, instead of the moulded plastic one supplied in the kit today. He fitted a dethermaliser to prevent fly-aways, mounting the fuse near the centre of gravity; this avoids trim changes with differing fuse lengths, which might alter the balance and act as a rudder if fitted at the rear of the fuselage.

Cutting Wood

Some of the sheet balsa parts in your kit may be die-cut, but it is still sensible to ease them out of the sheet with a scalpel as some wood fibres often still bridge the die-cut line. When cutting balsa do not simply press down with the blade; this will crush the wood instead of making a clean cut. Instead, draw it quite gently along the line to be cut, taking several light strokes instead of trying to cut through in one pass. Keep the blade vertical to the wood surface, and steady the wood firmly on your cutting board, close to where you are cutting. Never cut towards your fingers, and try to steady your cutting wrist on the board. Be aware of the wood grain, which may divert the blade from the line you intend to cut along. Practice cutting on some scrap balsa to get the feel of accurate working.

Use a steel straightedge or safety ruler to cut straight parts. If you are cutting a curve, try to make the first cut outside the printed outline, and then trim accurately once the component is free of the wood. If there are both internal and external curves, cut the internal one first. On hard balsa make short cuts at the start and finish of the curve, working towards the middle. Be careful of splitting off small projections.

Use your sanding block to trim each part to the final shape. Stick abrasive paper round a suitable dowel or bottle for an effective shaper for concave curves.

Do not cut on the plan. Use a 6 × 6 inches (150 × 150 mm) offcut of ply or board as a firm surface. Some people use a piece of thick card on this, which saves the scalpel tip from blunting. Better still, use a graphics cutting mat. When cutting soft and fragile wood, use a new blade. Keep your old blades; they can still be used for cutting harder wood or ply, which will blunt the blade quickly.

First Steps

Spread the plan out on the board, after smoothing out any creases. To prevent the glue sticking the structure to the plan (unlike when you built the Darts), tape a sheet of waxed paper or cooking film over the plan. Failing this, rub each marked joint on the plan with a wax candle or a bar of soap; this, too, stops glue adhesion.

The *tailplane* is the best part to start with. If you are not satisfied with your work you can scrap it and try again without wasting too much effort. The structure of your kit may differ from the Ajax. Identify the leading and trailing edge wood, and very lightly sand each surface to remove any saw marks, which weaken the wood. Hold it on a flat surface while you do this, and always sand only *away* from where you are steadying the wood, or it will break. Pin the outline in exact place on the plan, with pins each side of the wood strip, rather than through it, which weakens the wood. Pin the mainspar in place if there is one.

The tailplane of the Ajax has ribs which must be shaped after gluing in place, and the instructions in the kit on this are poor. Cut lengths of ⅟₁₆ inch (1.5 mm) balsa slightly longer than the ribs. Lay one on top of the wood on the plan and mark where it crosses the spar, by looking vertically down on it and making two light scalpel cuts. Lay the rib 'blank' on your cutting board and finish the cuts. Make the third cut, using a piece of the spar wood as a guide for the correct depth (see A). Return the blank to the spar, fit it on and in the same way mark with the blade where it must be cut to fit the leading and trailing edges. These cuts may need to be slightly angled to match the sweep of the leading edge. Glue the rib in place and repeat for the others.

Add the tailplane tips. Let the glue dry completely and unpin it from the board. Using a scalpel to remove light shavings at first, and then the sanding block, trim the ribs to the profile shown on the plan (see B). Hold the tailplane close to the edge of your board for this, so you can shape the trailing edge to the correct tapered section. Round the leading edge in the same way. Using light, circular sanding movements helps to prevent damage during this process.

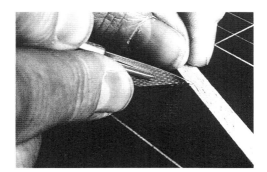

When cutting, hold the wood firmly down, close to where you will cut it. Always use a very sharp blade. Hold the scalpel like a pencil and *never* cut towards your fingers.

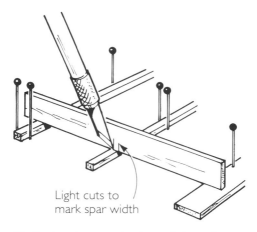

When cutting an inside curve like this, use several light cuts, and cut halfway round the curve, starting from each end. Cut the outer convex side last, and be careful not to split the acute angled corners where the wood grain runs crosswise.

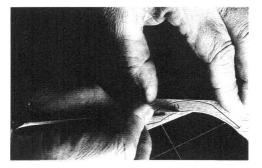

Light cuts to mark spar width

A) Cutting the spar slot in a tailplane rib blank. The overlength blank has been placed over its position on the plan and the spar location lightly marked with the scalpel. These marks are then fully cut with the blank removed to the cutting board.

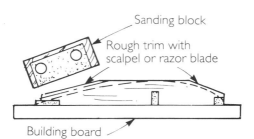

Sanding block

Rough trim with scalpel or razor blade

Building board

B) After the tailplane rib blanks are glued in place and dry, the corners are roughly trimmed down with the scalpel or a razor-blade.

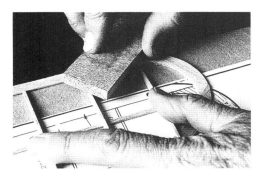

The tailplane is held down at the edge of the building board while a sanding block is used to shape each rib, along with the leading and trailing edges. Use light strokes, and sand away from where the part is held, rather than backwards and forwards, to avoid buckling it.

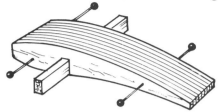

C) When the wing ribs are removed from their sheet, stack them together and slip a length of scrap spar wood through the spar slot to hold them aligned. Tap them down gently on a flat surface and then pin the block of ribs together before lightly sanding them to identical size.

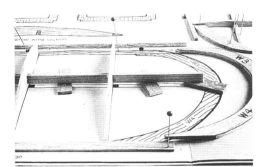

Small pieces of scrap balsa are used to raise the mainspar from the plan so it lines up correctly to the undercambered wing ribs.

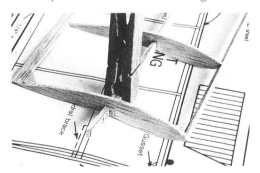

A clothespeg or bulldog clip is used to hold the dihedral brace to the spar while the glue dries.

The *fin* is made in a similar way.

You may find that your kit has a solid sheet balsa fin and tailplane. This may have anti-warp keys let into it at right angles to the spanwise grain. When you glue these in place lay a sheet of cooking film over it and place a heavy book or other flat object on top to hold the assembly flat while the glue dries.

The *wing* will have ribs either die-cut or printed on sheet balsa. Cut these out and stack them into a block, tapping them on a flat surface to ensure they are even. Slip a short piece of wood the same section as the mainspar through the spar slot to align them, pin the stack together from both sides, and lightly sand the top and bottom surfaces to make sure all are identical and smooth (see C).

Pin down the leading and trailing edges and the spar. If the wing is undercambered you will need to support the spar above the board on small pieces of packing. Glue the ribs in place; those at the wing roots or at the dihedral breaks may need to be set at an angle when seen from the front. Wipe off any surplus glue round each joint to minimise the weight. The leading edge may be square wood set at 45°. In this case it is best to add it after the ribs are in place, holding the strip snugly into the notches cut into the leading edges of the ribs with pins pushed into the board.

A dihedral brace will probably be used to reinforce the break in the mainspar at dihedral joints. In the Ajax instructions there is no mention of the need to cut a wider spar slot into two ribs to take this. Glue one end of the brace into place, holding it with a bulldog clip or clothes peg till the glue dries. Slip the other wing panel on to the brace and check the fits at the ends of the leading and trailing edges and spars. Sand these to fit exactly. Then glue the panels together, with one pinned to the board and the other blocked up to the correct dihedral angle. A small piece of masking tape may help to hold everything in place temporarily.

The centre section may be covered with thin sheet balsa. Cut this to exact size on the structure rather than the plan to allow for the curve. Lightly damp the outer surface of the sheet. This will make the grain swell and encourage the wood to curve away from the damped side. Glue and pin it into place.

The *fuselage* must be strong enough to withstand the tension and twisting of the rubber motor, and absorb shocks of landing and hard impacts. It also has to position accurately the wing and tail, the noseblock and the thrustline of the propeller shaft. (*Continued on page 80*)

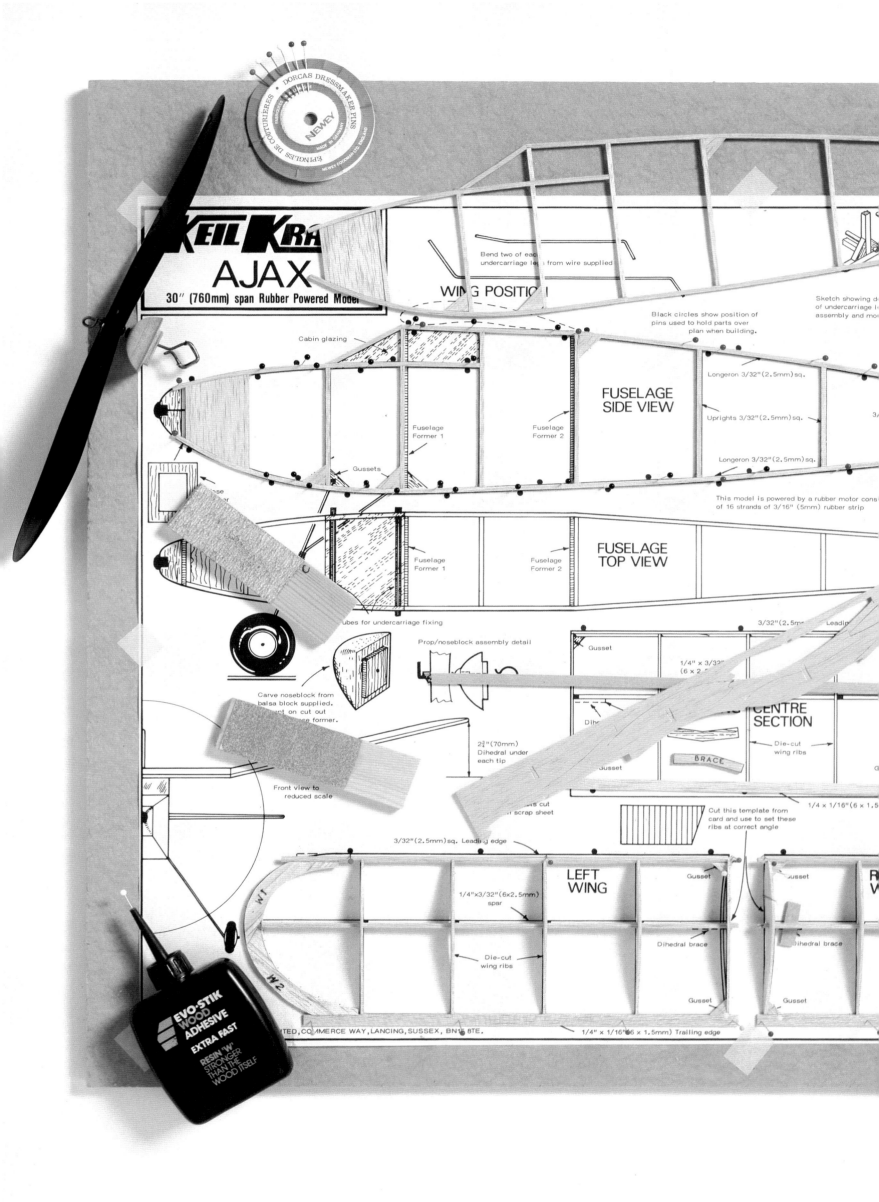

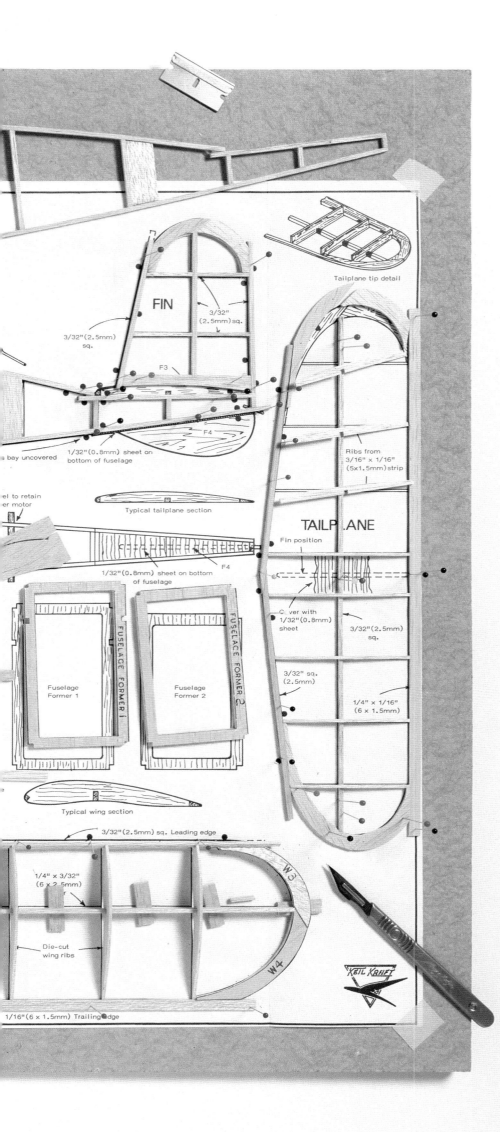

FIN

3/32"
(2.5mm) sq.

3/32" (2.5mm)
sq.

F3

F4

s bay uncovered

1/32" (0.8mm) sheet on
bottom of fuselage

el to retain
er motor

Typical tailplane section

Tailplane tip detail

Ribs from
3/16" x 1/16"
(5 x 1.5mm) strip

TAILPLANE

Fin position

F4

1/32" (0.8mm) sheet on bottom
of fuselage

C ver with
1/32" (0.8mm)
sheet

3/32" (2.5mm)
sq.

Fuselage
Former 1

FUSELAGE FORMER 1

Fuselage
Former 2

FUSELAGE FORMER 2

3/32" sq.
(2.5mm)

1/4" x 1/16"
(6 x 1.5mm)

Typical wing section

3/32"(2.5mm) sq. Leading edge

1/4" x 3/32"
(6 x 2.5mm)

W3

Die-cut
wing ribs

W4

KEIL KRAFT

1/16" (6 x 1.5mm) Trailing edge

BUILDING ON THE BOARD

The Ajax begins to take shape. The plan is taped down flat on the building board, but the clear plastic film, used to prevent parts from sticking to the plan, has been left off for the photograph.

One fuselage side is already finished, and the other is drying on the plan, with large-headed pins each side of the longerons to hold them in place. The two formers that will space the sides apart at the front and rear of the wing are cut out and notched to receive the longerons. The plastic propeller has been fitted to its shaft and the noseblock; plastic tubing round the propeller shaft hook prevents damage to the rubber motor.

Both the wingtips are drying on the plan; note the small pieces of balsa packing to raise the spar off the board to meet the undercambered ribs. Half of the tailplane ribs have been fitted; when all are in place and the glue is dry, the upper front and rear corners will be roughly trimmed and then sanded carefully to an airfoil section.

Two balsa sanding blocks are on the left, with different grades of garnet paper stuck flat on to them. These homemade 'tools' are among the most useful in the model-builder's armoury. A plastic bottle of white PVA wood glue is at the lower left; a handy tip is to remove any excess from round a joint before it dries, using a pointed scrap of balsa strip. This keeps the weight down, and avoids rough blobs of hard glue spoiling the tissue covering and impeding the sanding.

A sharp-bladed scalpel is to hand; many builders keep a fine oil stone handy to keep the blade ultra-sharp for accurate cutting. At the top is a single-edged razorblade.

The important thing is not to hurry. It is far easier – and a lot more satisfying – to make a joint right the first time than to try to correct it later.

On simple aircraft, the fuselage consists of four longerons running fore and aft, one at each corner, joined into a box with uprights and cross braces to resist buckling. External formers and thin stringers can be added to give a curved surface or a streamlined nose entry. Select the straightest and most evenly matched pieces of stripwood for the longerons. Steam two of them to match the sharp curve of the lower nose. Wear gloves to protect your hands, and ease the wood into the right shape. Check it frequently against the plan and when satisfied hold it in shape till it cools.

Pin two strips down on the plan, projecting at the front and rear. Use plenty of pins on the inside of the steep curve near the nose. Pin close to each upright, but not directly in line, as this will interfere with the wood when you are cutting it to length. When you cut the uprights, use any harder wood for those at the front, so as to keep down the weight at the rear. Start at the deepest part of the fuselage, so if you cut a piece too short it can be used elsewhere.

It is simplest to build the second fuselage side on top of the first, so cut the uprights in identical pairs, using the first as a template to cut the second. Glue the first set into place.

Add any sheet reinforcement to the nose area and for the rear motor peg, and any gussets for the wing dowels or undercarriage fixing.

When the first side is dry, thread the second pair of longerons into position over the first. Glue in the uprights and leave until the glue is set fully. The pins can then be removed, and the sides lifted off the board and separated by carefully sliding a razorblade between each joint.

An alternative method is to remove the first side from the plan by removing the pins from the lower side of each longeron, leaving the others in place. Pin the second set of longerons in position, using the same set of pinholes.

To join the sides, permanent formers may be used in the design, with notches in each corner to locate the longerons. Alternatively, you can make temporary ones from strip balsa as shown, to hold the sides square and in the correct position while the horizontal spacers are fitted (see D). Before using either, make sure that there is no excess glue in the corners in which they will be fitted.

Line up the two sides at the front and clip them together. Glue together at the tail, inserting any spacers shown on the plan; on some designs, the sides come directly together at the rear. Clip the tail end together to hold the sides aligned.

Unclip the nose and glue the nose former, probably of ply, into place. Bind and glue two or three turns of cotton round the outside of the nose and hold this from slipping off with pins.

Add the permanent or temporary formers at the front and rear of the wing position to hold the sides apart and square. Glue in the rest of the spacers, after cutting them to the correct length in pairs over the top view of the fuselage. Use light rubber bands to hold the sides together. You may find it easier to invert the fuselage on the board and use blocks of scrap balsa to hold it in place over the plan, to prevent it becoming banana-shaped .

When the glue is dry, add the sheet panels to the top and bottom of the nose bay, and add a fillet of glue inside each corner to strengthen this area. Cut off the longeron projections and remove any temporary formers you used.

The *noseblock* supplied in most kits is a square block of balsa. If you do not have a drill-stand you will need to mark the front and rear faces of this and drill carefully halfway through from each side, using a small diameter drill. The holes should meet in the middle, but if not run the drill or a thin Abrafile by hand through the holes to line them up and then enlarge the hole to take the plastic nose bearing supplied in most kits today. This bearing should be epoxied into place, but can be dislodged in a heavy landing. It is better to use a brass or aluminium tube, epoxied in place, or, better a brass bush.

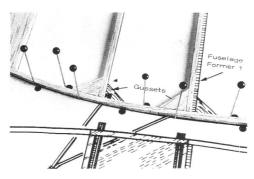

Large-headed pins either side of the balsa fuselage longerons hold them in place on the plan during assembly. Sharp curves may need steaming to shape to avoid straining the wood and producing distortions.

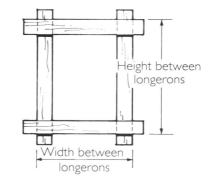

On the Ajax two formers hold the two fuselage sides apart at its widest point. They are a permanent part of the structure.

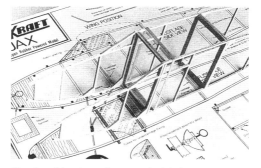

Height between longerons

Width between longerons

D) Sometimes false formers like this may be used to hold fuselage sides square to each other and the correct width apart. They are removed or cut away after the spacers are glued into place.

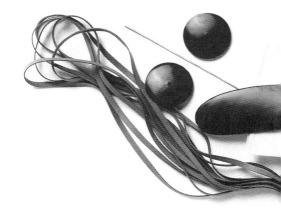

Another type of false former, of thick card or balsa, with notches at each corner for the over-length longerons, holds the two sides in position at the nose while the spacers are glued in place. Pins hold the longerons temporarily to this former and a few turns of thread are wrapped round the nose as well.

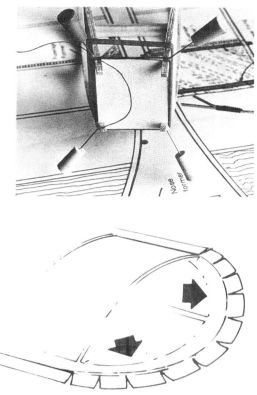

E) Wingtips may need covering with a separate piece of tissue. After the piece is pasted or doped to the outermost rib, gently stretch it away from this rib as shown till it is reasonably tight and can be stuck to the tip. Notches then cut into the tissue outside the wood form flaps which can be doped or pasted neatly underneath.

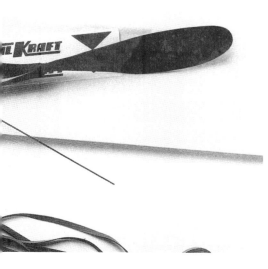

To prevent wear of the noseblock glue a 1⁄64 inch (0.4 mm) ply facing to the rear. This avoids changes in the thrust line as the wood compresses.

Covering is much simpler than you might think. First, lightly sand the entire structure and make sure that there are no protruding blobs of glue. Give it a coat of clear dope, thinned 50 per cent, and sand again lightly when it has dried. Make sure that the wing and tail assembly fit snugly in place and line up squarely, but do not glue any of the wing attachment dowels in place yet, as they make the fuselage harder to cover.

Your kit will probably contain a sheet of a rather porous-looking tissue; this is easy to use and repair, but absorbs rather a lot of dope. Later you may prefer to use a Japanese-made tissue, less porous and thus finally lighter.

The covering adhesive can be thinned wallpaper paste; add a few grains to an eggcup-full of water and it will swell to a sticky gel that weighs almost nothing when dry. Many people today prefer to use clear dope to stick tissue.

Start with the bottom of the fuselage. Cut some tissue ½ inch (15 mm) or so larger all round than the part to be covered. Apply the paste or dope to the edges of the part only, except later when you cover the undersurface of the wing, when the undercambered ribs will also need adhesive.

Hold each end of the paper and lower it on to the sticky surface. Starting at the middle gently stretch the tissue across the width of the fuselage and press it on to the paste or dope. Work out to each end, pulling lightly in a herring-bone fashion away from the first area you stuck. Using a small brush, apply a little more dope where it looks dry; it will quickly soak through the tissue and bond to the wood, so you can do this on the surface. Just get the covering reasonably wrinkle-free, and don't be afraid to get a little dope on your fingers. Cover another part or the opposite side of the fuselage while the first surface dries.

When it is dry, trim off the surplus tissue. Using a fine sanding block like a file, very lightly sand through the tissue along the corners of the structure and the excess will drop away.

Use a separate piece of tissue for the top of the wingtip. This has a compound curve that is hard to cover in one piece, so cover the wing up to the final rib, and then finish the wing with the last piece. Some people lap the tissue over the tips by about ¼ inch (6 mm). In this case, cut the tissue to this after it is stuck and cut darts in the surplus every ½ inch (15 mm) or so (see E). Lap these over and dope or paste down, smoothing them down well.

Let the paste or dope dry completely. Water-spray the tissue, using a scent spray, household spray or, as a last resort, by getting a nail brush and drawing your thumb across the bristles. Holding the part in the steam from a kettle works, too. Don't soak the tissue, but simply dampen it. Be careful of touching wet tissue, though, as it has little strength in this state. When it dries, the tissue will tauten. When it looks dry, put the wings and tail on a flat board and weight them down at the edges to dry out fully. This can take a day or so. Weighting down a wing like that of the Ajax, with three dihedralled panels, is tricky. The best scheme is carefully to spray one panel at a time, and weight that down for a day before doing an adjacent one.

Doping should be done in a well-ventilated room. Model flyers love the smell of dope, but not everyone does, so do not fill the house with fumes. Choose a warm, dry place; moist atmosphere causes the dope to 'blush'; this white discolouration mars the appearance, but does no harm, and can be removed by re-doping with a coat of thinners in a dryer place. In any case, thin the dope about 50 per cent or more as it will warp the flying surfaces if used straight from the can. Dope one flat panel at a time; on the Ajax for instance, the left tip, the centre section and finally the right tip. As soon as the dope is dry to the touch, pin that panel down and leave overnight before repeating the process for the other panels.

When the dope has dried and the wings and tail have been pinned flat for several days, it is time to prepare and inspect them. If the fixing dowels in the fuselage were left out to ease covering, install them now. Fasten the wing and tail with rubber bands and ensure the fin is pointing exactly along the centre of the fuselage. Check from the front that the wing is parallel to the tail. If not, glue paper or thin ply strips under the side that needs raising.

Install the rubber motor, propeller and undercarriage, so the model is ready to fly. If the centre of gravity is marked on the plan, balance the model with your fingers under the wing at the right place and either slide the wing fore and aft or add weight to the nose or tail till the Ajax balances horizontally. If no cg is shown, balance on the mainspar.

Trimming Before test flying, wait for a calm day and choose a field with long grass to soften landings. Always launch into the breeze. Test glide by launching the model with a gentle push towards a point on the ground about 30 feet (10m) away. The action should be like a slow-motion dart throw. The model should float away and land on an even keel. If the model dives steeply, move the wing forward about ⅛ inch (3mm) and launch it again. Repeat this till the glide is correct. If the wing is fixed, add 1/32 inch (0.8mm) packing under the tailplane edge instead.

If your model stalls, either add ballast to the nose, move the wing back slightly, or add packing under the landing edge of the tailplane. Make any trim adjustments one at a time, and check their effect, so you will know which change altered the model's flight.

When the glide is satisfactory, wind fifty turns on the propeller in a clockwise direction seen from the front. The model should fly straight and level till the motor runs out. Increase the turns in steps of fifty; the model should fly 50–100 feet (15–30ms).

Now the model is flying safely under power you need turn to make the model circle and reduce the distance it flies. The normal flight pattern for a model with a freewheeling propeller is right under power and right on the glide. For the model to circle the fin should be moved so that 1/16 inch (1.5mm) of the right side is exposed to view when looking down the centre line from the front. If the fin is fixed, glue a short strip of 1/16 inch (1.5mm) balsa down the righthand of the trailing edge and trim the length to adjust the circle. You may prefer to make a small trim tab from masking tape, as with the Dart. Vary these adjustments to make the required turn.

Try 100 turns again. The model should fly a semi-circle on both power and glide. Keep the turn quite open, about 100 feet (30m), to avoid excess banking. Increase the turns. If the model does not climb, move the wing forward or add packing under the tailplane trailing edge. Increasing the turns increases the torque from the motor, which rolls the model left; move the thrust line to the right to counter this. A piece of 1/64 inch (0.4mm) ply glued to the left rear side of the noseblock is the answer.

With still more power the model will fly faster and the wings produce more lift; a full stall may not occur, but the climb may be a series of zooms and swoops. To cure this, pack the top of the noseblock down with thin ply, angling the thrust line downwards.

When you go to the flying field take a scalpel (poke the blade into a piece of scrap balsa block for protection, or make a sheath from card and masking tape) and balsa cement for repairs and for gluing in the packing strip. Include several thicknesses of balsa and ply, modeling clay ballast, spare rubber bands for the wing and tail, masking tape and a winder.

A model may be be damaged or collect tissue tears. Tears are simply repaired on the field by drawing the edges together and running a thin bead of cement along the tear. As it dries, it shrinks and pulls the tear together; larger holes may be mended by doping a patch of tissue in place. You may want to make a neater job at home by cutting out the damaged bay and re-covering it. Structural damage is best repaired at home. Flying surfaces can be pinned on the board and the broken wood repaired either with splints, tapered off each end to avoid a sudden stress raiser, or by splicing in a new length of wood, with a long, angled Scarff joint.

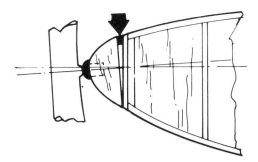

F) To adjust the climb under power, up- or down-thrust can be added by gluing small strips of thin hard balsa or ply to the rear of the noseblock as shown.

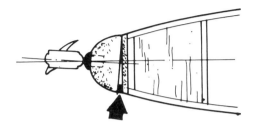

G) Climb turn adjustments can be made by altering the side-thrust in a similar way

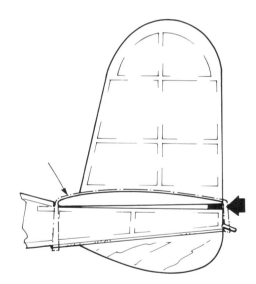

H) If the aircraft dives on the glide the tailplane incidence angle can be reduced by gluing balsa strip under the trailing edge. Use small variations, about 1/32 inch (0.8 mm) at a time. A glide stall can be cured by adding the strip under the leading edge.

GOING FURTHER

Johannes Graupner is a major German manufacturer of model flying equipment, kits and parts. Since 1955 the company has organised an annual competition for under 16s flying the Kleine Uhu (Little Owl) glider, kitted by Graupner, with major prizes for national and regional winners. Over 60,000 boys and girls enter, and the competitions introduce many young Germans like these both to model flying as a challenging and exciting sport, and to a career in science and technology.

The far-sightedness of Graupner, supported by the Uhu adhesive company and the German Aero Club, has done much to popularise model flying in Germany. Many towns have a dedicated model flying site, and it is included as part of schools' science teaching programmes. Unfortunately no British company has followed

Graupner's initiative, so model flying, science teaching and kit sales in Britain suffer as a result.

The Kleine Uhu in the picture (above) is an early version. Today the competition uses a radio-controlled glider and an electric-powered kit, as well as an improved free-flight version of the glider.

This Ascender, built by Spencer Willis, is an intermediate rubber model kitted by the New Zealand company Airsail. Its folding propeller gives a better glide than a freewheeler. The Ascender is unusual in having twin fins and a single leg retracting undercarriage.

Westwings produces the kit for this F-117A Nighthawk 'stealth' aircraft. It can be flown either as the catapult glider shown here, or as a rubber model with a motor stick and propeller added.

Stefan Gasparin produces this jewel-like Taylor Cup Peanut scale model as a part-finished kit. With a wingspan of only 13-inches (330 mm), the kit includes the completely assembled balsa structure, ready for tissue covering, as well as moulded plastic wheel shells and cowling. It is intended for the Gasparin G-10 CO_2 motor, but can be converted to rubber power.

The Senator, designed by Albert Hatfull, is kitted by Keil Kraft in Great Britain and has a 30-inch (762 mm) wingspan. It is a good follow-up model from the Ajax, with an impressively steep spiral climb and a startlingly good performance, making it a good introduction to competition flying.

The Senator has a freewheeling propeller and a single leg undercarriage; this one was built by Spencer Willis.

BUILD A FLOCK OF FOAM FLYERS

Intended to be built cheaply and in quantity, from a roll of polystyrene household wall insulation, this simply-constructed little glider is a real 'floater'. Designed by Robin James, it cleverly utilises the natural curve of the foam roll to form the aerofoil section of the wing. A simple stick fuselage gives rigidity and the use of card templates to cut out the parts makes mass production easy. Build several and have great flying fun with your family and friends.

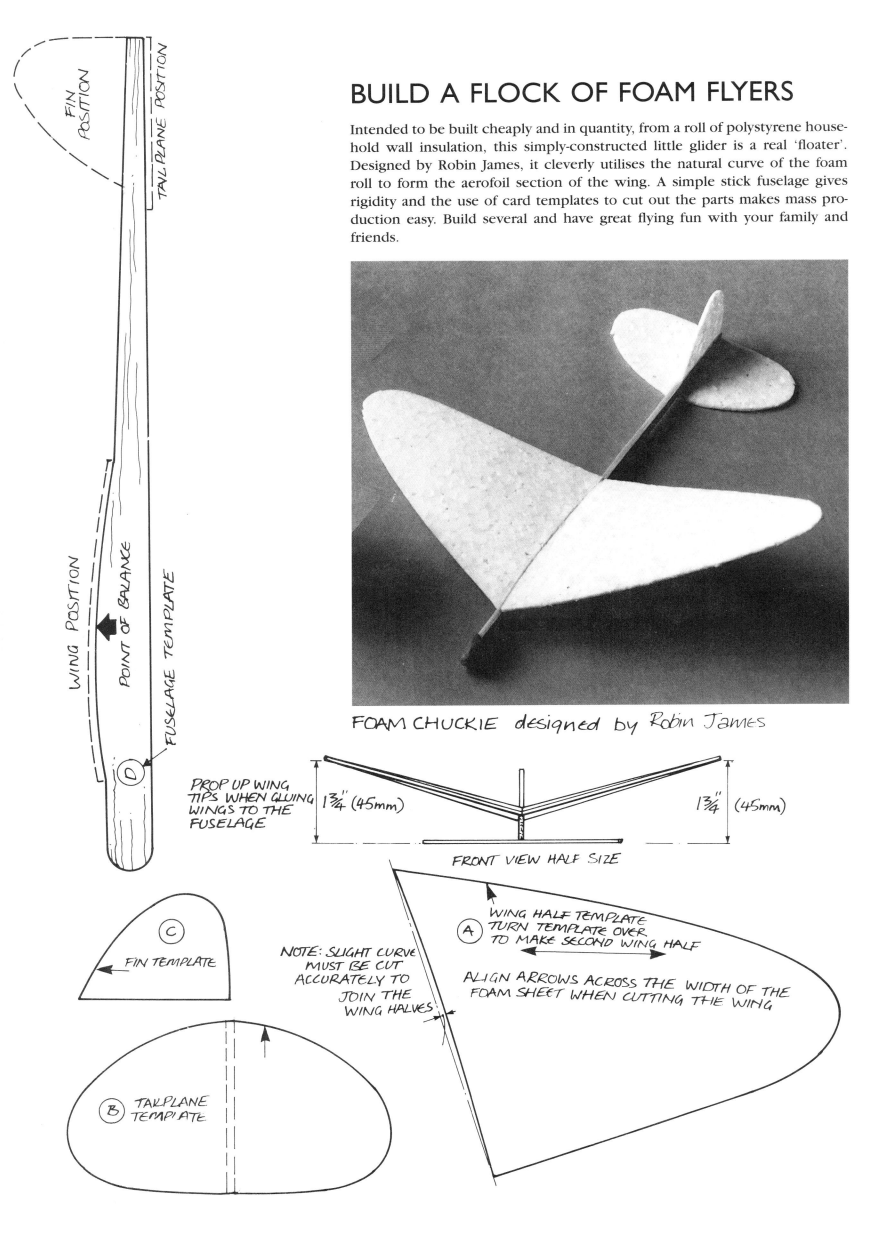

FOAM CHUCKIE designed by Robin James

FRONT VIEW HALF SIZE

1¾" (45mm)   1¾" (45mm)

FIN POSITION

TAIL PLANE POSITION

WING POSITION

POINT OF BALANCE

FUSELAGE TEMPLATE

D

PROP UP WING TIPS WHEN GLUING WINGS TO THE FUSELAGE

C   FIN TEMPLATE

B   TAILPLANE TEMPLATE

NOTE: SLIGHT CURVE MUST BE CUT ACCURATELY TO JOIN THE WING HALVES

A   WING HALF TEMPLATE TURN TEMPLATE OVER TO MAKE SECOND WING HALF

ALIGN ARROWS ACROSS THE WIDTH OF THE FOAM SHEET WHEN CUTTING THE WING

BUILDING THE 'FOAM CHUCKIE'

MATERIALS YOU WILL NEED

An offcut or roll of 2 mm polystyrene foam wall insulation, available from most DIY stores. One sheet of ³⁄₃₂" (2 mm) straight grained medium weight balsa sheet, available from model shops. A glue suitable for polystyrene, such as R/C Modellers' Glue or Copydex; do not use balsa cement, as it will melt polystyrene. A small amount of modelling clay for balancing, and a piece of thin card-board for making the templates. You will need a sharp modelling knife, a straightedge and a building board or cutting surface. Adhesive tape and pins will also be useful. Study the plan and instructions carefully.

1 Photostat or trace the template drawings A, B, C and D shown on the opposite page.

2 Lightly glue your copy of the template drawings onto thin cardboard; the thickness of a cereal packet is ideal. Cut out the shapes accurately, following the thicker continuous line, not the dotted lines which show assembly positions.

3 Cut a 3" (155 mm) length from the roll of polystyrene foam sheet and, with the natural bend in the sheet face down, fix with tape onto a cutting surface.

4 Use card template A to cut out one half of the wing. Then turn the template over to cut the other half. Check the wings are cut across the foam sheet in order to create a curved aerofoil section along the length of the wing.

5 Use templates B and C to cut out the tailplane and fin from the foam sheet.

6 Use template D to mark out with pencil the shape of the fuselage on the balsa sheet. Cut out this out using a straightedge ruler on the long sections; cut carefully round the curves.

You should now be ready to assemble the model. Note the small arrows which indicate the front or leading edges of the wing, tailplane and fin.

7 Firstly, glue the tailplane in position underneath the rear of the fuselage as indicated by the dotted lines on the plan. Then glue the fin vertically on the top of the end of the fuselage. Hold in position till the glue dries, being sure to keep the fuselage upright.

8 Glue the two halves of the wing together onto the curved section on the top of the fuselage as shown on the plan. It is most important to form the angle or 'dihedral' at the same time. You will need to prop up the tips of the wing on each side by 1¾" (45 mm) as shown in the front view diagram. Use tape or pins to hold the two wing halves together onto the fuselage while the glue sets thoroughly.

9 Before flying balance the model. The balance point, or centre of gravity is halfway along the wing joint as shown on the plan. Add modelling clay to the front of the fuselage until the model rests horizontally when balanced on your fingers under the mid-point. Finally check the model from the front to ensure the dihedral is correct and that there are no warps in the wing, tailplane or fin. These can be bent out with slight finger pressure.

10 For indoor flying, launch the model gently with the nose pointing slightly down. Outdoors on a calm day launch more strongly and level into the breeze. If the model persists in diving, bend up the rear or trailing edge of the tailplane. If it zooms up and stalls, bend the tailplane trailing edge down slightly. Adjust turns with the fin. Have fun!

Powered Foam Flyers

Above Steve Midson designed this rubber-powered Cabfly for quick building from thin polystyrene foam sheet which weighs a fifth as much as balsa. Based loosely on the Auster series of post-War British light aircraft, a Midair kit is available for this 13" (330 mm.) wingspan indoor flyer. Use a roll of wall insulation and design your own when you have some experience with Midair flyers. The lightness and resilience of this material is the secret of success for these aircraft.

Right The Midair Tradfly is an all-foam kit with a 13" (330 mm.) wingspan, based on the pylon type of engine-powered free-flight duration aircraft. Steve Midson's kit designs weigh about ⅓ oz. (10 grammes), and are capable of half minute flights indoors, or outdoors on a very calm day.

Right Microfly is another Steve Midson foam polystyrene kit. It has a 14" (350 mm.) wingspan and looks like the Thruster microlight. With its low centre of gravity and high-mounted wing it is ultra stable in flight. Midair kits are available by post from Midair Models or SAMS; both addresses are in the suppliers' list on page 96.

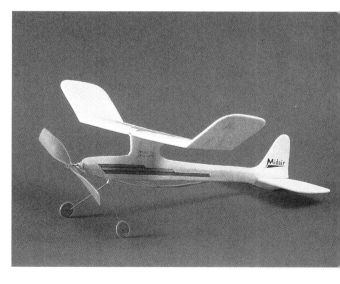

MEMORIES OF EMPIRE

Bill Lewis built this GB-2 twin-motored flying boat in 1992. With a 47-inch (1,194 mm) wingspan, the H.S. Sayers design first appeared in *Aeromodeller* magazine in the early 1940s.

The two carved balsa propellers rotate in opposite directions to cancel out the effect of the rubber motor torque, which would tend to make the aircraft roll. The two nacelles, each containing a rubber motor, are held to the wing with rubber bands to reduce the risk of damage in a heavy landing.

Taking off from a portable water-filled pond of polythene sheet, this model managed flights of over 60 seconds during a vintage contest at Middle Wallop, England, in 1992.

Perhaps inspired by thoughts of the Short Empire class passenger flying boats that plied the long-range routes of Imperial Airways, or of the record-breaking Supermarine S-6B seaplane that was a forerunner of the Spitfire, rise-off-water contests had a considerable following in Britain till about 1950.

World record classes for rubber- and engine-powered model seaplanes exist today. The current duration and height record-holder, Boris Krasnorutski, and the aircraft he used are shown on page 94.

Left Winding the GB-2 is a two-stage affair. A purpose-built 'stooge' holds each motor nacelle as its rubber motor is stretch wound. After winding the first its propeller is held locked by a pin system while number two motor is also wound.

Right Imperial Airways long-distance passenger routes relied from 1937 very largely on the Short Empire flying boat. Powered with four radial engines, flights from Britain to Australia took several days including overnight stops along the route.

FASCINATING FLAPPERS

Since earliest times man has been fascinated with bird flight. Many unsuccessful experiments have been made to achieve this; Leonardo da Vinci designed wing flappers, but may not have actually built one. The high-energy storage of the simple rubber motor has meant that, today, skilled modellers have managed successfully to fly model ornithopters, but to do so takes considerable expertise and dedication.

John White's experience with rubber-powered ornithopters spans more than 40 years. Most early model ornithopters used a single pair of beating wings; this caused a lot of vibration and wasted about half the available rubber motor energy.

In 1954 John developed the biplane ornithopter, based on the dragonfly; its wings beat out of phase and thus greatly reduced the vibration, allowing the whole aircraft to be built lighter. That year, at Hawker Aircraft's old airfield at Langley, west of London, he set a British duration record of 1 minute 55 seconds.

As well as the cranks through which the rubber power flaps the wings, there are other critical parts of a successful ornithopter. The wing leading edges must be light but must also resist vertical and horizontal bending, as it is these spars that transmit the energy to the flexible wing, and in turn carry the lift loads. The shape and tension of the tissue that forms each wing is also important, for it must curve into an efficient airfoil, rather like a single propeller blade, while being billowed by the air pressure it creates as it flaps.

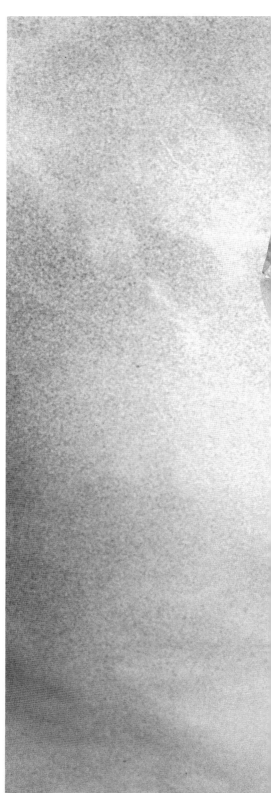

Front view drawing of the wing-flapping crank mechanism of John White's Flapjack model, showing wing spars in the open position. Power is 12 strands of ¼ inch (6 mm) FAI Supplies rubber.

John White's 1992 biplane Flapjack ornithopter design is available from *Aeromodeller*'s Plans Service. Wingspan is 40 inches (1,016 mm) and weight 2½ ounces (70 g). John has also built a smaller indoor version.

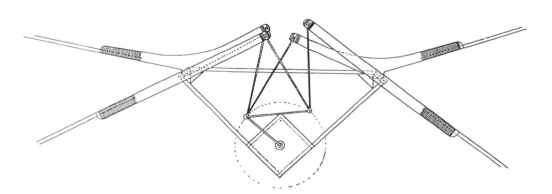

John White launching his Dragonfly ornithopter on its record-setting duration flight in 1954 during the Northern Heights Club Gala at Langley.

Left Contests for rubber-powered helicopters took place until about 1970. This *Aeromodeller* magazine cover shows Ian Dowsett launching his large design. The rubber motor drove rotors at each end of the fuselage, with stabilising fins to prevent the fuselage itself from rotating too. The climb was vertical, to several hundred feet, and a freewheel system allowed the rotors to auto-rotate to slow the descent when the power ended.

Right Another moving-wing aircraft is the autogiro. Unlike a helicopter, its rotor blades are not power-driven, but spin in the airflow produced as the autogiro is pulled forward by its propeller. This Peanut scale model is a Cierva type of the 1930s, built by Pete Smart.

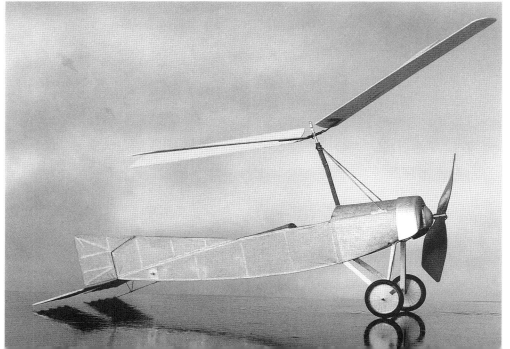

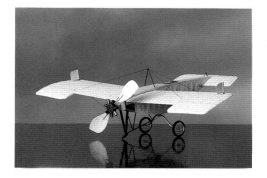

Chris Hutchinson's 1911 Bleriot Type 25 is a Peanut class indoor scale model, with a 13-inch (330 mm) wingspan. A rotary engine powered the original, driving a pusher propeller at the rear; the seven cylinders were attached to the propeller and rotated with it, causing gyroscopic problems when the pilot wanted to turn the aircraft. Chris's rubber power avoids this difficulty. Yaw control on this aircraft came from the two rudders mounted near the wingtips.

Full circle

The European Fighter Aircraft is jointly produced by Britain, Italy, Spain and Germany. Like the earliest powered aircraft, EFA has a canard foreplane, but in this case it is used to increase manoeuvrability at high speed and high angles of attack, and not for stability; the aircraft could be flown in steady flight without it. Computer-controlled fly-by-wire techniques make such flight systems possible, as the control would be too sensitive for a human pilot to operate directly.

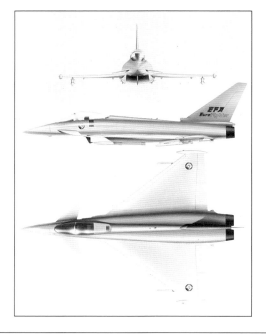

Fourteen-year-old Alan Hardwick took the fourth place at the 1992 International Vintage Contest at Gorizia, Italy, flying this PEG 54 A-frame, designed in 1924, over 50 years before he was born.

The wing and foreplane are held to the fuselage frame by rubber bands. The propellers revolve in opposite directions to cancel the tendency of the rubber motors' torque to roll the model. Some A-frame flyers use a converted hand-cranked egg-whisk to wind both motors at once, but make sure you do it the right way round. Having your model fly backwards when you launch it can be quite a surprise.

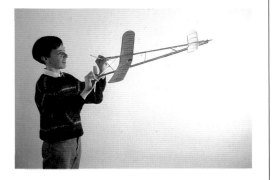

Alan Hardwick demonstrates the launching technique for a twin propeller A-frame pusher. This type of model was popular till the mid-1920s, and competitions were held for distance as well as for duration. A firm, slightly nose-high launch is important, and releasing both propellers at once takes some practice.

PUSHING ON

When Orville Wright made the world's first controllable powered flight in the United States in 1903, he and his brother Wilbur used a canard or tail-first design. They thought this gave a more rapid pitch control response, and the same layout was favoured by other pioneers such as the French Voisin brothers and Henri Farman. Many model aircraft also flew with a foreplane, rather than the tailplane usual today.

A canard arrangement was used by the Soviet-designed Tupolev 144, an aircraft similar to Concorde, and by several of the revolutionary US home-built glass-fibre and carbon composite types developed by Bert Rutan, such as the Vari-Eze and the Vari-Viggen. Rutan is yet another model flyer who has made a major contribution to full-size aircraft design.

Pusher propellers, rather than the more usual tractor type, have been used for several reasons. The airflow behind a propeller is very turbulent, and moves backwards in a fast spiral. Placing the propeller behind the flying surfaces ensures that they are not affected by this, and are instead flying in smooth air. A disadvantage is that engines are quite a heavy part of the aeroplane, and should therefore be near or in front of the centre of gravity; a pusher propeller requires a long shaft from the engine to drive it, and this adds weight and may increase vibration.

Some fighter aircraft of the First World War, such as the De Havilland 2 and the FE 2b, had a pusher propeller and engine mounted at the rear of a central nacelle, with twin booms either side of it attaching the tail assembly to the wing. This allowed the gunner, sitting precariously in the nose, a clear field of fire. When interrupter gear was developed to allow machine-guns to fire through the propeller disk, tractor propellers came into their own.

PRIME SITES

Every sport has its Meccas. Mention Taft, in the Californian semi-desert, to a free-flighter and his eyes will probably go a bit starry. This vast flat area is clear for four or five miles, except for scattered tumbleweed and the odd rattlesnake. Taft lies midway between San Francisco and Los Angeles, was the site of the 1979 World Free-Flight Championships, and has been the focus of US competition flying for decades. In the summer it gets hot, more than 40 degrees is common, and some flyers carry small survival packs at their waists: compass, space blanket and Gatorade to replenish their rapidly evaporating body salts in case of a mishap downwind while retrieving a long flight.

In Britain Old Warden, 50 miles (90 km) north of London, is owned by the Shuttleworth Collection and is the venue for nostalgic full-sized flying displays in the summer. Many unique vintage aircraft inhabit its hangars. Model flyers, too, with a passion for pre-1950 designs, gather for similar meetings; the atmosphere is relaxed and there is as much talking and reminiscing as flying. Simply being there is enough, with the models that belonged to the time when aviation wasn't the dirty word it often seems to be in the complaint-ridden Britain of the 1990s.

The annual high-point for many European flyers is Les Journées Internationales de Vol Libre en Poitou, better known simply as 'Poitou'. This event is part of the FAI's sporting calendar, and is held over huge fields of maize and sunflower stubble in rural France, 50 miles (90 km) south of the Loire valley. The farmers welcome the flyers, the flyers pray that their models stay out of the surrounding fields of still-standing sunflowers and maize, reaching well above man height. Watching the models through binoculars as they circle in thermals, there always seems to be a ravishing view of some fourteenth-century Romanesque church, an abbey or château, shimmering in the heat. This, too, has been a World Championship site, in 1987, when 35 nations competed for the Wakefield Trophy.

For free-flight enthusiasts the tragedy of Yugoslavia has been a double tragedy. Several major championships have been run on the superb dry lake-beds near Mostar and Livno, in now-ravaged Bosnia. Hundreds of flyers remember the magical mix of mosques, markets, modellers and mountains. Driving out from Mostar in 1980, through the arid white limestone karst mountains, on the winding, sun-bubbled tarmac road, the first sight of the 14-mile (23 km) long field of Mostarsko Blato was like a glimpse of paradise. A few cows tended by weather-beaten old ladies in black were grazing on the short grass of the vast pasture, and some models were already testing the air, as the morning mist burnt off in the sun. Little did we know. Will there ever again be such a peaceful scene there?

Indoor flyers in Britain have the immense Cardington airship sheds near Bedford for their activities. Built in the 1920s to house the huge R100 and R101 airships intended to be used on long-range commercial air routes, the twin sheds have a ceiling towering 164 feet (50 m) and are 900 feet (275 m) long.

They are listed buildings, protected by law, and regarded by indoor flyers almost as if they were a religious edifice. Inside they feel like one, too; with sunbeams angling down

Most competition model flyers use a stopwatch, a pair of lightweight binoculars, a good marching compass and a large-scale map of the area. Getting a precise compass bearing on the landed model and following it accurately prevents losses.

through the windows high up near the roof girders they certainly have a cathedral-like air about them, and the sort of aircraft that fly inside look miraculous, too.

A thousand miles away in Romania the saltmine at Slanic is another focus of indoor flying. Reached via a hair-raising lift that drops flyers and their boxes 600 feet (190 m) into the bowels of the earth, the mine is very cold, only just above freezing, and flyers wear anoraks to keep warm while competing. The huge saltcave has dim lighting and rough walls; touching one with a microfilm model can be a problem, as they tend to stick.

OUT AND RETURN

Having been launched into the perfect thermal, your aircraft will be some way downwind in a few minutes, and you want it back. Most competitions require several flights, each of a maximum time of usually three minutes. This minimises the effect of the lucky monster thermal, à la Korda in 1939.

But first, it must come down. To upset the carefully-adjusted aircraft enough to bring it down fast but safely takes something drastic. A dethermaliser, usually a steeply tipping tailplane, does the trick. On some light models the entire wing pops off, to flutter round on a line attaching it to the back of the fuselage. Triggering it takes either a slow-smouldering fuse of lampwick, with its unlit end held by a metal snuffer tube to prevent fires, or a lightweight clockwork timeswitch; there are now electronic timers to do the job, too.

With the model down, there are some aids to recovering it. Brightly-coloured wing, tail and fin tips, contrasting with the natural surroundings, make it easier to spot. While it is coming down, watch it carefully, if possible with binoculars, and note exactly what landmarks are on the same line from you. Contest flyers use a marching compass, as used by orienteers, to take a bearing on the model when down; take a reciprocal back-bearing upwind of you, and note a landmark there,

too. As you walk towards your model it is surprising how the downwind horizon features change, so a back-bearing can help.

Follow your compass line exactly, taking frequent checks on your bearing. If you need to cross a wood, identify a tree on the exact line, maybe only a few yards away if the wood is dense, and walk to it. Repeat this careful check, tree by tree, until you leave the wood, and you will still be on the correct line. When you are in the area you expect the model to be, look upwards in trees as well as on the ground and behind bushes or in long grass. Climbing a tree helps to give a better view of the surroundings.

Today's free-flight aircraft may carry ultra-light radio tracking beacons, like those used for following wild animals, or else audio bleepers. If the model is up a tree you will find a bow and a weighted, de-feathered arrow useful. Attach the tail of the arrow to some nylon fishing line and shoot it over the branch to shake the model gently free. If needed, the nylon line can be used to pull a heavier rope over to shake thicker branches.

If at first you cannot find the model, begin a square search. Mark a bush, perhaps with a shirt; then move 10 or 20 yards (10–18 m) across wind from it and follow the same compass line back upwind till you are sure you are out of the area where the model could be. Repeat this, crosswind again, then back downwind on the line till you spot the model. Occasionally an air search is needed for the tougher cases. Sometimes, finding your free-flight model after a flight can be fraught with unexpected incident.

During the 1977 World Championships at Roskilde in Denmark Martin Dilly was downwind helping the short-handed Hungarian F1C team. It was a hot day and he had his shirt off. Looking upwind for the next model to be launched he rested his elbows on a fence to steady the binoculars. A second later he had two black eyes as the jolt from what turned out to be a particularly vicious electric fence banged the binoculars hard into his face.

At the same championship the North

Korean team had the use of their embassy's Mercedes car to follow models. The chauffeur at one stage was seen driving the car straight through a field of tall maize, with a Korean flyer standing on the car boot for a better view. Definitely *not* the way to improve relations with the local farmers.

The 1963 World Championships were held in Austria, at Wiener Neustadt airfield, vacated a few years before by the Soviet air-force, and before that heavily bombed by the USAAF. One edge of the field had an area roped off with a warning of uncleared landmines.

In Australia during the 1983 World Championships at Goulburn, one hazard waiting for models gliding downwind was a group of large, aggressive, white-backed magpies the size of crows. They rose like interceptor fighters and attacked models that came near their nests.

In Armenia, during the Soviet Championships in the 1980s, Evgeni Verbitski, one of the all-time greats of F1C flying, was looking for a model in some dry rocky country. Jumping over a wall, he landed on a snake, which promptly bit him in the leg. Soon he began to feel very ill, but managed to get back to a dirt road; he flagged down a passing truck, which took him off to hospital where he stayed for several weeks recovering. Had he not been found by the truck, doctors told him he would probably have lost the leg.

The acres of maize and sunflowers at Poitou make retrieving there hazardous. Finding a model can be a big problem, and it is important to take a very accurate compass bearing from the launch point to where the model lands. That at least gives the direction, but not the range. A cross-bearing from a different place is even better; where the lines cross you find the model. However, finding the *person* is harder. The trick is for him to have a walkie-talkie and a brightly-coloured hat. He walks carefully into the field, invisible to the watchers outside. Once in, he raises his hat on the end of a tall maize stalk till it can be seen. The two people with the compass bearings then talk him by radio on to the lost model by 'steering' the hat to where the lines cross.

If a model is lost in dense undergrowth, climb a nearby tree to spot it from above. Persuade a friend to fight his way into the gorse, brambles, poison ivy or whatever and direct him to the model by watching the movement of the vegetation as he struggles through.

Whatever you do, make sure you put your name and address on all free-flight aircraft. The labels often ask the finder to place the model where it can be easily seen by searchers. One British flyer failed to find his glider after a long flight from a Lincolnshire airfield. Rain set in and he went home. Some months later another flyer searching for his own model in the same area asked at a farmhouse. The farmer showed him into a barn where the other model rested, bleached and badly warped. Following the label, he had thoughtfully tied it to a fence with binder twine, where it had stayed for several weeks in high summer.

SAFETY

Compared with many sports, model flying is very safe. However, take a few sensible precautions before you launch that new model.

First, *think*! Where will the wind take it? Is there a road, railway or anything else downwind where the sudden arrival of a model air-craft could cause a problem? Are there people near where you intend to launch, just in case the model is not yet flying correctly? Launch well downwind of them. If you are flying a towline glider, make sure the line is not inconveniencing other people.

If you use a fuse-type dethermaliser, always use a snuffer tube. In some countries this type of D/T is banned in the dry season.

If your aircraft lands in overhead wires, do not try to recover it; even low-level electricity lines on wooden poles carry lethal voltages.

The operator of any aircraft, even though it's unmanned, is subject to Article 51 of the Air Navigation Order. This states: 'A person shall not recklessly or negligently cause or permit an aircraft to endanger any person or property.'

Remember: *Safe Flying is No Accident*.

WEATHER

Because the aircraft they fly are very light and fly slowly, free-flighters soon become conscious of small changes in the local climate. Wind strength and direction are important. The models always drift downwind after launch, even though they are adjusted to circle, so always pick the upwind side of the site to launch from. Beware, though, of buildings, trees and other obstructions further upwind of you. The wind, blowing over and round these, produces turbulence for a long way downwind of them, which can easily upset a model aircraft.

Launch directly into wind; many people use a light streamer on a pole to observe the exact wind direction before launch. Wait till there is a lull in the breeze, and watch indications such as waving grass and bushes upwind of you to see if the lull persists. Try not to choose a spot with tall trees or houses downwind of you, too; your model has to arrive safely back on the ground, as well as flying.

The heart of free-flight is the thermal. This is a patch of air warmer than its surroundings that therefore rises; launching into this 'lift' boosts the flight time, but detecting it is quite a subtle skill.

A thermal forms when a patch of air is slowly warmed by the sun on the ground, and breaks away as a large rising bubble, moving off with the wind. The cooler air surrounding it then moves in to fill the lower-pressure area produced by the departure of the thermal. In Norway an annual contest is flown from a frozen lake; even on a freezing cold day some of the air is slightly warmer than its surroundings, and therefore rises. On a summer day every fluffy cumulus cloud marks the top of a thermal, and are sure to bring a smile of anticipation to glider pilots.

One way of feeling a thermal is to wait till the air warms slightly (the arrival of the core of the thermal) and to launch when the breeze starts shortly afterwards (the upwind edge of the thermal, or 'fill'). This, with luck, ensures that as your aircraft climbs and starts to turn, it will be drawn into the rising air.

Other means exist for spotting 'lift'. A pole-mounted light Mylar streamer, 30 or 40 feet (10 or 12 m) long, both shows the wind direction and also indicates a thermal by pointing upwards towards the rising air. At a big contest 20 or 30 streamers flutter in the breeze, like the pennants on jousting knights' lances.

Some flyers use automatic soap-bubble blowers upwind; the rising cloud of shimmer-

This tripod-mounted thermal detector plots a trace of small changes of air temperature on a chart on a slowly rotating drum. A highly sensitive electronic thermometer is mounted several metres up on a fibreglass pole, and its amplified output drives the pen making the trace. Flyers usually launch when the temperature is high and the wind speed has been low for some time.

ing bubbles makes a useful visual marker for a good patch of air. Specially-saved bulrush fluff, like thistledown, can also be used. Simply watching for insects being lifted upwards, or for swallows circling high to catch them, helps. Gulls, storks, vultures and buzzards are past masters at thermal spotting. Other airborne models are good 'lift' indicators; all are pre-adjusted to fly in circles, both to keep them in the air they are launched into, and also to stay in sight of the timekeepers.

Perhaps most effective is the sensitive electronic thermometer. This shows very small changes in air temperature (half a degree is significant), and a slow steady rise marks the arrival of a thermal; connected to a chart recorder this provides a visual trace on paper to show the pattern of thermal development. Sometimes a similar device plots windspeed, too; when the paper traces show a rise in temperature and a drop in wind, a thermal has probably arrived.

Swiss Wakefield flyer Roger Ruppert uses a thermal detector with twin traces plotting temperature and wind-speed changes on the same moving chart. The electric outputs from the wind and temperature sensing heads at the top of a pole attached to the device power two modified radio-control servos that drive the plotting pens.

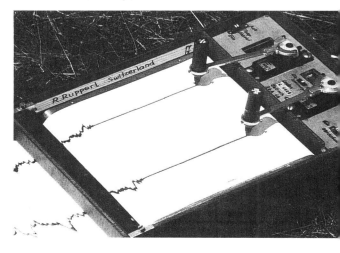

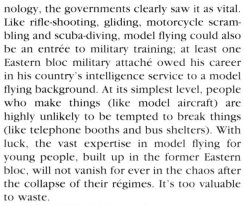

EVENTS AND CONTESTS

Free-flight enthusiasts all over the world have a huge range of events and competitions to enjoy, outdoors in the summer and indoors in the winter when the weather is cold and blustery. The easiest way to find where the fun is, is to look in the 'What's On' pages in the magazines and free-flight newsletters, or contact your national model flying organisation. There are a few fixed points, though.

In Britain the National Championships (The Nats) take place on the three-day Spring Bank Holiday at the end of May. The venue is usually RAF Barkston Heath, near Grantham, used during the week by student pilots from the RAF college at Cranwell who are learning to fly Tucano trainers; this is now the most important site for free-flight in Britain and the local site for flyers from 100 miles away. The Nats consists of about 27 contests for almost every type of free-flight aircraft, and is a fine introduction to the sport for visitors.

If it's a jamboree atmosphere you want, rather than people enjoying modern competition flying, then one of the Old Warden days organised by ASP, who publish *Aeromodeller* magazine, may appeal. Old Warden is in Bedfordshire. There sometimes tend to be rather too many radio-controlled power models cluttering up the sky for some people's taste, flown with more enthusiasm than skill, so perhaps the vintage competition organised by SAM 1066 at Middle Wallop airfield, near Andover, will be more to your taste. This event is usually on the three-day August Bank Holiday weekend, and is acquiring quite an international reputation. As well as the contest, you can enjoy the Museum of Army Flying, also on the airfield.

Local leisure centres see low-key indoor flying, with models from Peanut scale to EZB, and even indoor radio-controlled models, powered by CO_2 motors. Centres at Crawley and Watford are ones to watch; spectators are welcome in the galleries, and many a karate enthusiast or trampoline jumper has stopped to watch, fascinated by a sport very different from his own.

Official Support and Funding

In many countries model flying receives financial support from several sources. National teams and flyers at World Free-Flight Championships have been aided by firms like Volvo, Land Rover, UHU, Aérospatiale and British Aerospace. In Britain the sport is recognised as such by the Sports Council, and all the former Eastern bloc countries provided extensive state funding.

The sport was seen as a double benefit to the country. At one level it caught the imagination of young (and not so young) people in a technical-oriented activity where their own initiative and skill showed in the results. As a stepping-stone to a career in science or tech-

nology, the governments clearly saw it as vital. Like rifle-shooting, gliding, motorcycle scrambling and scuba-diving, model flying could also be an entrée to military training; at least one Eastern bloc military attaché owed his career in his country's intelligence service to a model flying background. At its simplest level, people who make things (like model aircraft) are highly unlikely to be tempted to break things (like telephone booths and bus shelters). With luck, the vast expertise in model flying for young people, built up in the former Eastern bloc, will not vanish for ever in the chaos after the collapse of their régimes. It's too valuable to waste.

In the USSR, DOSAAF, the government air sports organisation, ran frequent training camps for young model flyers, and two-week selection programmes to pick national team members were held in a warm part of the country every spring. Records were seen as very important. Near Dnepropetrovsk in the Ukraine regular sessions were run with the aim of capturing particular world records, and the results paid off. Fifteen out of the 27 outdoor free-flight records are held by flyers from the former USSR, and all but one of the rest by people from other socialist states.

Helicopters tracked models launched for distance and height records. The rules for rubber-speed records require models to fly a 328-feet (100 m) course in both directions within half an hour, to minimise the effect of a tail wind. The fastest aircraft are really rubber-powered projectiles, designed to fly straight, and to survive the hard arrival at the end of the run. Hand-launching is allowed; a liberal but effective interpretation of this lets the flyer launch the aircraft a bit like an Olympic hammer throw, with a sling that starts the propeller as the model is accelerated. Andrei Belanov's 116 mph (187.68 km/hr) record was the result.

Clubs and More

Worldwide

Model flying, which is now the world's most popular air sport, is far more enjoyable with other people to help and advise you. Internationally the Fédération Aéronautique Internationale is air sport's equivalent of the International Olympic Committee. FAI commissions exist for every air sport from ballooning to hang-gliding, and advise on matters concerning their speciality. For model-flying it is the CIAM (Commission Internationale d'Aéromodelisme) that does the work; about 30 nations are represented at its meetings in Paris, making it by far the biggest pool of model flying expertise that ever gathers in one place. This shared experience helps model flyers worldwide, you included.

The FAI organises World and European Championships for every type of model flying, indoor and outdoor, free-flight, radio-controlled and control-line, at which teams from many nations take part. Well over 100 FAI Open International contests are run as well, in which thousands of individual model

flyers compete from all over the world.

As well as a quarterly magazine, *Air Sports International*, the FAI publishes *CIAM Flyer*, an annual magazine with a strong accent on model flying for beginners, and of particular interest to teachers. Copies cost $3.00 and can be obtained from the FAI, at 10–12 rue du Capitaine Menard, 75015 Paris, France.

Your National Association

In Britain, the British Model Flying Association is responsible for every aspect of the sport. Like the British Parachute Association and similar groups for gliding, ballooning and so on, the BMFA is given this task by the Royal Aero Club, and is recognised by the Sports Council.

There are 530 BMFA clubs in Britain, with around 28,000 members, flying everything from 1-gramme microfilm aircraft to radio-controlled scale models weighing 30 pounds (13 kg) or more. A phone call or a letter to the Association (Chacksfield House, 31 St Andrews Road, Leicester LE2 8RE, tel: 0533 440028) will put you in touch with a club near you; as a BMFA member you will receive a handbook covering all general aspects of model flying, with competition rulebooks filling in the rest of the detail. A regular specialist newspaper, *BMFA News*, also goes direct to every member.

As well as looking after safety, noise, flying sites, national and local legislation, radio frequencies, airspace, piloting standards and so on, the BMFA provides members with a unique third-party insurance; there are also over 150 BMFA events organised for members. It is the BMFA which selects the teams that represent Britain at Championships, and runs the education scheme for young model flyers, using the BMFA Dart as its core; teachers' packs on the scheme are available.

Two British chapters of the Society of Antique Modelers exist for people interested in models designed before 1951:

SAM 35 (some radio-control activity), Hon. Sec. Les Duffy, 9 Queens Road, Wellington, Somerset TA21 9AW.

SAM 1066 (no R/C), Hon. Sec. David Baker, 24 Pinetrees, Weston Favell, Northants NN3 3ET.

USA

In the USA the Academy of Model Aeronautics has around 172,000 members in 2,400 clubs, and is a division of the National Aeronautic Association. It offer benefits similar to those of the BMFA, and lays great stress on supporting education. As well as classroom packages to enhance students' learning opportunities in science and maths, the Adopt-a-School program encourages liaison between schools and AMA clubs. The Renaud Research Library is a major source of aviation reference material, and a large range of AMA promotional and instructional videos on the sport is available. Membership includes the monthly 150–200 page magazine *Model Aviation*. The AMA's address is 5151 East Memorial Drive, Muncie, IN 47302; tel: 93170 289-4236.

Society of Antique Modelers, Sec. Bob Dodds, 209 Sumerside Place, Encinitas, CA 92024.

REAL AERO CLUB DE ESPAÑA
Miembro Fundador de la Fédération Aéronautique Internationale

Bulgaria
Bulgarian Federation of Air Sports
75 Vasil Levski Blvd
1040 Sofia
Canada
Model Aeronautics Association of Canada
Unit 9
5100 South Service Road
Burlington
Ontario L7L 6A5
Chile
Federacion Aerea de Chile
Jose Arrieta 7698-B La Reina
Casilla Postal 1074
Santiago
Croatia
Hrvatsky Zrakoplovny Savez
Dalmatinska 12
41000 Zagreb
Czech Republic
Ceskomoravsky modelarsky svaz
Miroslav Navratil
U Pergamenky 3
170 00 Praha 7
Denmark
Kongelig Dansk Aeroklub
Lufthavnsvej 28
DK–4000 Roskilde
Estonia
Eesti Lennuspordi Foderatsioon
Mesika 30
EE0020 Tallinn
Finland
Suomen Ilmailiitto
Helsinki-Malmin Lentoasema
SF-00700 Helsinki

France
Fédération Française d'Aéromodelisme
52 rue Galilée
75008 Paris
Germany
Deutscher Aero Club
Rudolf Braas str. 20
6056 Heusenstamm
Greece
Greek Aeromodelling Federation
PO Box 31986
GR-100 35 Athens
Hungary
Magyar Modellezes Szovetseg
Pf. 614
1374 Budapest
India
Aero Club of India
Safdarjung Airport
Aurobindo Marg
New Delhi 110 003
Ireland
Irish Aviation Council
c/o Kenneth Townsend
The Old Cottage
Rathdawn Road
Greystones
Co. Wicklow
Israel
Aero Club of Israel
67 Hayarkon Street
PO Box 26261
Tel Aviv 63432
Italy
Aero Club d'Italia
Via Ferruzzi 38
00143 Roma

Japan
Nippon Koku Kyokai
18–2, Shimbashi 1-chome
Minato-ku
Tokyo 105
Korea
Dai Han Hang Kong Hyup Hwae
CPO Box 3855
132–5 1-Ka, Bongnae-Dong
Choong-Ku
Seoul
Latvia
Latvian Aero Club
Spilves Iela 1
226007 Riga
Liechtenstein
Modellfluggruppe Liechtenstein
Schaanerstr. 112
FL-9494 Schaan
Lithuania
Lietuvos Aeroklubas
Sporto 34
2051 Vilnius
Luxembourg
Fédération Aéronautique Luxembourgeoise
BP 131
L-2011 Luxembourg
Mexico
Federacion Mexicana de Aeronautica
Puerta 9 Ciudad Deportiva
Magdalena Mixhuca
Despacho 325 3er. Piso
CP 08010 Mexico, DF
Netherlands
Koninklijke Nederlandse

Vereniging Voor Luchtvaart
Jozef Israelsplein 8
2596 AS S'Gravenhage
New Zealand
New Zealand Model Aeronautic Association
PO Box 918
Wellington
Norway
Norsk Aero Klubb
PO Box 3869 – Ulleval Hageby
0805 Oslo 8
Pakistan
All-Pakistan Aeromodelling Association
17 A KDA Scheme No. 1
Karachi 5
Poland
Aeroklub Polski
Krakowskie Przedmiescie 55
00–071 Warszawa
Portugal
Aero Club de Portugal
Rue General Pimenta de Castro 4 C
1700 Lisboa
Romania
Federatia Romana de Modelism
Str. Vasile Conta 16
70139 Bucharest
Russia
National Aero Club of Russia
88 Volokolamskoye sh.
123042 Moskva
Slovakia
Zvaz modelarov Slovenska
Jozef Gabris
Wolkerova 4

800 00 Bratislava
Slovenia
Letalska Zveza Slovenije
Lepi Pot 6
PO Box 496
61001 Ljubljana
South Africa
South African Model Aircraft Association
PO Box 39071
Garsfontein 0042
Spain
Real Aero Club de España
Carrera de San Jeronimo 15
28014 Madrid
Sweden
Sveriges Modellflygforbund
Box 100 22
600 10 Norrköping
Switzerland
Aero Club der Schweiz
Lidostrasse 5
CH-6006 Luzern
Turkey
Turk Hava Kurumu
Ataturk Bulvari 33
06100 Opera/Ankara
Ukraine
Federation of Aeromodelling Sports of Ukraine
Industrialnaya 27
252056 Kiev
Venezuela
Asociacion Venezolana de los Deportes Aereos
Apartado 50088
Caracas 1050 A

Left A world speed record of 116.2 mph (187 km/hr) for rubber-powered aircraft was set by Andrei Belanov of the Soviet Union in 1987. Two flights must be made in opposite directions, to cancel the effect of wind. The aircraft was hand-launched, from a fast run up, with a device to lock the folding glass-fibre propeller until free of the hand, and a site was chosen to allow a landing on water to minimise damage. The model, more of a projectile than an aircraft, had a dural tube fuselage and was powered by a 9½-ounce (270 g) motor. Three men were needed to hold the model and one to restrain the flyer winding it.

Below left Boris Krasnorutsky of the Soviet Union set a world duration record for rubber-powered seaplanes in 1987 using this 77-inch (1,960 mm) span aircraft, powered by a 5.6-ounce (160 g) rubber motor. A world altitude record of 3,750 feet (1,143 m) was also set on the same flight.

SOME FREE-FLIGHT WORLD RECORDS

Glider

Duration	M. Milutinovic	Yugoslavia	4h 58'10"
Distance	Zdenek Taus	Czechoslovakia	310.33 km
Height	Gyorgy Benedek	Hungary	2364 m

Rubber-powered

Duration	Vladimir Fiodorov	USSR	1h 41' 32"
Distance	G. Tchiglitsev	USSR	371.19 km
Height	Vladimir Fiodorov	USSR	1732 m
Speed	A. Belanov	USSR	187.68 km/hr

Engine-powered

Duration	Kulakowski	USSR	6h 1' 0"
Distance	E. Boricevitch	USSR	378.76 km
Height	Yin Chenbai	China	6468.9 m
Speed	A. Dubinetski	USSR	179.9 km/hr

Indoor (unlimited ceiling)

	Jim Richmond	USA	52' 14"

ACADEMY OF MODEL AERONAUTICS
1810 Samuel Morse Drive   Reston, Virginia 22090

FREE-FLIGHT SUPPLIERS

Advanced Model Composites, Unit 4, Halfpenny Bridge Ind. Estate, Oldham Road, Rochdale, Lancs OL11 1NS
Carbon and glass cloth

Aeromodeller Plans Service, Argus House, Boundary Way, Hemel Hempstead, Herts, HP2 7ST
Plans, including vintage

Aeromodel Mart, 165 Church Lane, London NW9
Model shop with useful range of free-flight needs

Aero-Model Sport, Wlodzimierz Mazurczak, 03–721 Warszawa, Ul. Jagielonsk 2/83, Poland
Timers, prop. hubs, blades, Wakefield parts

Aerospace Composite Products, PO Box 16621, Irvine, CA 92714, USA
Carbon-fibre strip

The Balsa Cabin, Unit 5, Mill Lane, Maldon, Essex CM9 7LD
Balsa, spruce and plywood

Bradley Model Products, 1337, Pine Sap Ct, Orlando, FL 32825, USA
Towhooks, timers

Champion Model Products, 880 Carfmen Court, La Verne, CA 91750, USA
Kits, scales, components

Composite Structures Technology, Dept B211, PO Box 4615, Lancaster, CA 93539, USA
Carbon and Kevlar parts, spares

DPR Models, Unit 9, The Vanguards, Vanguard Way, Shoeburyness, Essex SS3 9QY
Novelty and simple glider kits for young flyers

Duck Woods, 1285 N. Union Street, Stockton, CA 95205, USA
Balsa, spruce

Easy Built Models, PO Box 425, Lockport, NY 140-95-0425, USA
Manufacturers of beginners kits, including the Delta Darts with this book

Education Programme, BMFA, Chacksfield House, 31 St Andrews Road, Leicester LE2 8RE
Beginners' kits, teachers' packs for model-flying education programme

Engines from Russia, 100 Lowfield Road, Stockport SK3 8JR
Timers, prop. units and blades

Mike Evatt, 6 Armley Close, Long Buckby, Northampton NN6 7YG
Carbon and Kevlar cloth

FAI Model Supplies, PO Box 3957, Torrance, CA 90510, USA
Rubber

Vladimir Fedorov,
Федоров Владимир Александрович
Россия, Москва 115597
Гурьевский проезд
д19 кор2 кв.728   , Russia
Wakefield parts and mechanisms

Free-Flight News Supplies, 21 Ravensbourne Drive, Chelmsford, Essex CM1 2SJ
Rubber, timers, winders, towhooks, D/T fuse, hubs

Free-Flight Services, Gendalen 57, Furulund, 46694 Sollebrun, Sweden
Kits, wood, materials

Doug Galbreath, 2810 Chiles Road, Suite B, Davis, CA 95616, USA.
Timers

Bob Hatschek, 316 Grosvenor Street, Douglaston, NY 11363, USA
Circle towhooks

HI Models, Nad Prehradou 15, 321 02 Plzen, Czech Republic
Timers, carbon spars, towhooks, winches, booms, prop. units

John Hook, 42 Players Crescent, Totton. Southampton
Free-flight grade balsa, adhesives, tools, etc.

Mikhail Kochkarev, 125130 Moscow, Vokzalny 3–34, Russia
F1A glider towhooks, mechanisms, D-boxes, complete aircraft

Vladimir Manyshev, 143400. Russia (USSR)
Московская обл.
г. Красногорск, ул. Кирова 28, кв. 176
Манышеву Владимиру. (Manyshev Vladimir).
, **Russia**
Timers, propeller hubs, wing joiners

Joe Maxwell, 14 Upper Craigs, Stirling FK8 2DG, Scotland
Computer-machined wood ribs, wing forms, propeller blade blanks

Micro-X, PO Box 1063, Lorain, Ohio 44055, USA
Indoor balsa, bearings, kits

Midair Models, 97 Elmbridge Avenue, Surbiton, Surrey KT5 9HB
Rubber-powered foam polystyrene model kits

Model Produkter, Box 2060, S-87102 Harnosand, Sweden
Kits, timers, rubber, tissue

John O'Donnell, 20 Manderville Close, Winstanley, Wigan, Lancs WN3 6HL
Mylar film, carbon steel blades, soft soap, vintage magazines

Peck Polymers, PO Box 710339, Santee, CA 92072, USA
Kits for rubber-powered aircraft and plans

Ronytubes, 23 Ivy Road, Walkerville, Newcastle-on-Tyne NE6 4PU
Glass-fibre, carbon/glass motor tubes and glider booms

Paul Rowledge, 31 Portreve Close, Llantrisant, Pontyclun, Mid Glam. CF7 80W
F1C propellers, aluminium foil

Klaus Salzer, Darmstadterstr. 46, 6053 Obertshausen 2, Germany
Polyester covering materials

SAMS Models (Mail Order), The Chapel, Sandon, Buntingford, Herts SG9 0QJ
Free-flight materials, kits, rubber, CO_2 motors, books, plans, hardware, etc.

Hans Seelig, Mitterfeldstr. 1, 8930 Schwabmunchen, Germany
Timers

Sig Mfg. Co. Inc, 401-7 South Front Street, Montezuma, IA 50171, USA
Balsa and spruce, kits, dopes

Victor Stamov Production, 252134 Kiev, Simirenko 34–127, Ukraine
F1A glider timers, D-boxes, towhooks, booms, etc.

Starline International, 6146 E. Cactus Wren Road, Scottsdale, AZ 85253, USA
High-performance glider kits, towhooks

Jim Summersett, RT.4 Box 365K, Canyon Lake, Texas 78133, USA
Timers

Ed Turner, 3544 Granada Drive, Fort Worth, TX 76118, USA
Wakefield propeller units, etc.

W-Hobby, Acacialaan 29, 3730 Hoeselt, Belgium
Timers, towhooks and glider parts from Lithuania

Gerhard Wobbeking, Holstenstr. 108, 2000 Hamburg 50, Germany
Circle towhooks, components

Woodhouse Supplies, 12 Marston Lane, Eaton, Norwich, Norfolk NR4 6LZ
Carbon, Kevlar, glass cloth, tissue, rubber, plans, hardware, prop. units, etc.

NOW READ ON

Most information on free-flight is in specialist subscription newsletters and annual publications. These will help.

Aeromodeller, (monthly, newsagents)
ASP, Argus House, Boundary Way, Hemel Hempstead, Herts HP2 7ST

Airborne, RMB 1798, Samaria Road, Benwalla, VIC 3672, Australia

FFONZ News, (bi-monthly, on subscription)
18 McGeorge Avenue, Mornington, Dunedin, New Zealand

Free-flight, (monthly, included in NFFS membership) National Free-Flight Society, 12324 Percival Street, Chester, VA 23831, USA,

Free-Flight Down Under, (quarterly, on subscription) 46 Rondelay Drive, Castle Hill, NSW 2154, Australia

Free-Flight News, (monthly, on subscription) 7 Ashley Road, Farnborough, Hants GU14 7EZ

Model Aviation, (monthly on subscription, or free to AMA members) 5151 East Memorial Drive, Muncie, IN 47302, USA

Modelar, (monthly) Magnet Press s.p. Jungmannova 24, 113 66 Praha 1, Czech Republic

Modellbau Heute, (monthly magazine) Brandenburgisches Verlagshaus, Storkower str. 158. 0–1055 Berlin, Germany

Die Thermiksense, (newsletter, subscription) Fuchshofweg 25, W-7060 Schordorf, Germany

Vol Libre, (bi-monthly, on subscription; multilingual) 16 Chemin de Beulenwoerth, 67000 Strasbourg-Robertsau, France

BOOKS AND OTHER PUBLICATIONS

Aerofoils for Aeromodellers
Martin Pressnell (Pitman)

Aeromodeller Plans Handbook
(Argus Specialist Publications)

Building and Flying Indoor Model Airplanes
Ron Williams (John Murray)

Encyclopedia of Model Aircraft
ed. Vic Smeed (Octopus)

Free-Flight Forum Reports (from 1985, annually) (BMFA, Chacksfield House, 31 St Andrews Road, Leicester LE2 8RE)

Freiflug-Modellsport,
Dr Ing. Heinz Eder (Verlag für Technik und Handwerk GMBH)

Indoor Scale Model Flying Fred Hall

NFFS Symposium Reports (from 1968, annually) National Free-Flight Society, 1234, Percival St., Chester, VA 23831 USA

Indoor Model Building and Flying
Lew Gitlow (Indoor Model Supply)

Making Scale Model Airplanes Fly Pub. Aircraft Data, Dallas, TX 35376-3576, Model

Model Aeronautic Yearbooks
Frank Zaic (Model Aeronautic Publications)

Model Aeroplane Building Sketch by Sketch
Peter Holland (Argus Books)

Model Aircraft Martin Hedges (Hamlyn)

Model Aircraft Aerodynamics
Martin Simons (Argus Books)

The New Science of Strong Materials
J.E. Gordon (Pelican)

This is Model Flying Martin Dilly
(Elm Tree Books)

Peanut Power Bill Hannan (Bill Hannan)

Rubber Powered Airplanes Don Ross

The Science of Flight O.G. Sutton (Pelican)

Structures J.E. Gordon (Pelican)

World Free-Flight Review Vol. 1
William R. Harthill (World Free-Flight Press)

The World of Model Aircraft
Guy R. Williams (André Deutsch – Rainbird)